Endorsements for *the Pursuit of Porneia* and 423 Men

"Dave's Scriven's work with 423 has been the single most effective tool for sexual healing in our church, bar none. Hundreds of men have discovered freedom like never before. Not surprisingly, it's also one of the best spiritual formation tools I know of. Men come as sex addicts in isolation; they leave as disciples of Jesus in community."

John Mark Comer
Pastor for Teaching and Vision
Bridgetown Church, Portland, Oregon
author of *Garden City*

"I would always devour the 'Red Barron' report every time it was published. It was a classified document summarizing all the enemy aircraft activity and tactics in the last several months of combat. It was a must read because it came from the heat of battle and the front lines of the air war I was involved in at the time. It saved my life numerous times! Dave Scriven's book *The Pursuit of Porneia* is a spiritual Red Barron report for men. It comes from his experiences of leading 423 groups for years in the hand to hand combat of setting men free from the grip of sexual bondage. I love Dave's passion and honesty concerning the battles he has personally fought and won. I highly recommend this critical combat document. It is one of the best practical applications of the Pure Desire materials I have developed over the years."

Dr. Ted Roberts
Founder
Pure Desire Ministries International. Gresham, Oregon
author of *Pure Desi   )m*

D1441628

"When you've come to the end and realize you can't win the battle by yourself, this book, *The Pursuit of Porneia,* will give you hope. It's not only practical but is supported by Scripture. It's an honor to say that Dave has been my friend for thirty-five plus years."

Dick Iverson
Founder
City Bible Church, Portland, Oregon
author of *Building Churches That Last*

"Dave's heart and insights are invaluable, timely, and a necessary resource for equipping men to walk in holiness. *The Pursuit of Porneia* demonstrates that purity is not only necessary for spiritual maturity, but is the catalyst for discovering and unpacking our God given potential. Saturated in Scripture, deeply practical and personal, this book is a must read for any man desiring a closer walk with Jesus."

Dominic Done
Lead pastor
Westside A Jesus Church, Tigard, Oregon

"*The Pursuit of Porneia* is the right book for the right time. It uncovers the devastating effects of pornography on individuals and their relationships without pulling any punches, yet it offers hope for a way of escape. Speaking as one who has broken free of pornography's bondage, Dave Scriven offers a firsthand view of both the despair of addiction and the joy of freedom that can be found. Straightforward, insightful, and thought-provoking, this book is essential reading for anyone struggling with or who knows someone struggling with pornography."

Dr. Deborah J. Miller
Principal
Westside Christian High School, Tigard, Oregon

"In *The Pursuit of Porneia*, Dave Scriven describes emotional pain as a universal phenomenon. As a Professional Counselor and Marriage Family Therapist, I have the distinct privilege of sitting with individuals, couples, and families in the center of their suffering. Most of my clients can relate to the deep desire to medicate pain, sometimes with activities like shopping, food, work, or sex. Dave offers a clear and compelling explanation of the addictive process which keeps people trapped in the cycle of shame. His book is specifically intended for men who, in their attempt to escape intense emotional pain, became ensnared in the web of porneia. This book is a must-read for any man who wants to find healing in his struggle with sexual addiction."

Heather Anne Harrison MA, LPC, LMFT
Licensed Marriage and Family Therapist
Licensed Counselor, Beaverton, Oregon

"I have known Dave Scriven for more than ten years. I've watched his servant's heart as he volunteered, helping our custodial crew clean up after our Sunday gatherings. Later, I watched as he birthed and gave leadership to what has become one of the most important ministries of our church; 423 Men and 423 Women. Through '423 Communities,' hundreds of individuals have found healing from sexual addiction and gone on to live godly and pure lives. I watched Dave be a godly husband to his wife Adonica, who has now gone to be with Jesus. And I've watched him love and serve his children as a good and godly father. Dave is the real deal. He's a man of integrity who has been given a calling from the Lord Jesus, and who is faithfully carrying out that calling."

Phil Comer
Founding Pastor and Director of Intentional Parents
Westside A Jesus Church

"Dave Scriven gives men hope in this book, *The Pursuit of Porneia*. By vulnerably sharing his own story of sexual addiction and journey to recovery, Dave credibly speaks to men who are struggling and caught in the web of sexual sin, and gives hope and a path forward of how to overcome this prevalent issue among men – whether followers of Jesus or not. Dave's passion for seeing others freed from this addiction is evident in his actions personally, in how he leads 423 Ministries, as well as in the pages of this book."

Tony Viducich
Executive Pastor of Operations
Westside A Jesus Church, Tigard, Oregon

"423 is more than a program to help with sexual addiction... it is an amazing resource that leverages the power of confession and community to reform and rebuild the broken. It has created safe harbors of transformation in our church community and released men and women to bring that healing into their work places, schools and neighborhoods. It's been a gift to Westside."

Tim McDonald
Executive Pastor of Mission & Leadership
Westside A Jesus Church, Tigard Oregon

"After pastoring a church for twenty-six years in Dallas, Texas, I have yet to see a book so timely and relevant as *The Pursuit of Porneia* in confronting the wave of sexual perversion that is hitting the church with the full force of hell behind it. Dave has a God-given, personal revelation in dealing with issues of healing and deliverance, as well as the compassion and grace needed to offer hope to those who suffer with these chains of bondage... This book will change your heart."

Ray Galligan
Senior Pastor
Open Heavens Church, Garland, Texas

"The Pursuit of Porneia is a must read for anyone desiring sexual sobriety and a life free from sexual addiction. I have never read a book on this topic that is so well balanced with grace and truth. A book that does not focus on simply behavior and performance, but actually seeks to get at the heart and core of the issue of sexual addiction in a person's life. Practical, Biblically based throughout, and not a hint of shaming. Dave Scriven writes with genuineness and clarity, and this book reflects his character and integrity as a man who has personally been in the place of feeling hopeless, yet has found comfort and victory on the journey of freedom from sexual sin."

Micah Rydmark
Director
The Reality Project, Portland, Oregon

"Dave Scriven and 423 Men have brought hope and lasting change for hundreds of men struggling with sexual purity. In a culture that is increasingly becoming numb to porn and sexual sin, *The Pursuit of Porneia* is a must read for every man."

Gerald Griffin
Pastor of Communities and Leadership
Bridgetown Church, Portland, Oregon

"Dave Scriven's work in *The Pursuit of Porneia* is vulnerable, compelling and calls the reader to step into a deeper relationship with oneself and with Jesus. Accessible to anyone at any stage of the journey to freedom from sexual sin, Dave shares honest, gut-wrenching truth about loss, shame and the beauty of God's restorative power. Highly recommended!"

Phil Emery
Pastor of Worship and Support Groups
Mosaic Portland, Oregon

"Dave Scriven is making a lasting impact with this book and 423 Communities he founded to bring freedom from sexual bondage for men and women alike. In my own journey of healing, and with the leaders I've worked with, I've seen how secret sins holds us back from living the life God promises. We don't have to look far to witness how sexual abuse is ruining lives. One can suspect sexual addiction is at the heart of a problem that won't easily be solved without brave and humble leaders like Dave. In this book, he shares his own story and lovingly reaches out to those affected with a smart and effective way to fight the battle with Porneia. I highly recommend this book and the work of 423 Communities."

Larry Briggs
President and Founder
V2A Solutions, Tigard, Oregon
author of *Sticky Leadership*

"Dave Scriven has developed a unique sexual recovery model rooted in the last place many would expect to find it: the local church. *The Pursuit of Porneia* offers a powerful process for creating Christ-centered communities where sexual addiction loses its chokehold. But rather than putting more pressure on pastors and psychologists to pave the way, this book equips members of the church to minister to one another. Scriven's hard-won wisdom will encourage and educate those who are still stuck, as well as the leaders who care for them."

Andrew A. Boa
Founder
Strongholds, Wheaton College, Illinois
author of *Redeemed Sexuality*

THE PURSUIT OF PORNEIA

423 Men Member Reviews

"I feel that I have come a long way in the nearly three years I have attended group. I feel blessed that this opportunity came into my life as I truly feel it was pivotal in saving my marriage and myself from what felt like an unbeatable enemy… Thank you again for all the work you have put into building such a great resource for me struggling with sexual purity."

"In no other context in my entire life have I felt the ability to wrestle so deeply with my faith and learn what it means to walk with Jesus. 423 has made me significantly bolder in facing my problems…"

"Before 423 I didn't give a crap about following anything. I grew up in the church but… never experienced love through my shame… I would not be married if it were not for 423."

"Going into the group, I was struggling with looking at porn multiple times a day. I felt so disgusting because of my secret sin… I always asked myself, 'Why would God forgive me or want anything to do with me…?' Since entering the [423 Men] group, I have gone without porn or masturbation just under a year and a half…"

"I was always focused on fixing my sexual sin and since joining [423 Men] I've learned to fix my whole life around Jesus…"

"I feel equal to other people most of the time whereas before I felt like I was less than other people…"

"For 50 plus years, I have never been able to end my masturbation and pornography. I have been able to abstain for 15 months from everything except some double takes. Thank you God and thank you 423. I have never felt so close to God…"

"[423 Men] has been the most 'real' church that I have ever done."

"I have learned to focus on progress, not perfection, in effort to overcome the potentially devastating cycle of shame and its effects on our soul."

"…I am more often thinking of and talking to God now rather than of thinking of and fantasizing about sex/porn."

"I used be a hypocrite, going to church and pretending to be the good Christian that I wanted people to see. Now I am living a life of honesty and openness about my struggles and not putting on a mask for people."

"It [423 Men] has held me accountable for sexual sin. This has been where I have sinned more than anywhere in my walk."

"Being a part of a [423 Men] community has kept me from depression."

"A lot more aware of why I do what I do! And to know I'm not the only one dealing with it."

"Being free of my past addiction (pornography and masturbation) finally gave me the peace of mind that God was truly my Savior. Growing up a Christian I worried that my habitual sin would cost me my salvation…"

"There is no shame in group. I feel everyone there appreciates me regardless of what I tell them."

"I was addicted to pornography and was starting to make decisions that were escalating my addiction. I hit a point where I knew I needed help or else I would go completely over the deep end. Since finding and joining 423 I have started to learn who God is and his love for me…"

"I love having a place to come share big and small things that are going on in my life… it allows me to feel safe to share as well. As of right now there is nothing in the area of sexual addiction or root issues that I have felt I couldn't share with my group."

"...[My 423] group is a wonderful, open group of guys who have ALWAYS shown tremendous support and love for each other."

"Even in the most sensitive areas imaginable where I thought people would shun me for my past, I was surprised to find that my honesty was rewarded with grace and acceptance."

"I trust the guys in this [423] group more than anyone else..."

"There's nothing I can't share [at 423]."

"I realized that it was my secrets that were keeping me enslaved."

"I feel extremely safe in my 423 group."

"It honestly took about 2 years [in 423 Men] before I really saw a major change... My initial focus was to stop doing bad things (i.e., porn masturbation), but I am now focused on the true health and wholeness in the Lord (i.e., healthy sexual relationship with my wife, learning to trust others again, building lasting friendships, valuing intimacy over isolation). All along I've seen slow and steady gains in reducing the frequency of the times I 'act out,' but it has taken years for me to get to a place where I can learn to stop coping with life and start living with boldness and a fierce love for others."

"For the first time in my life, I feel God's grace. It is a great feeling and I thirst for more."

"Since joining 423 a year and a half ago, I have been porn and masturbation free. The first few months I was 'white knuckling' it because I didn't want to have to share that I had messed up with the group. After that, my heart began to change. Now, the reason I don't want to look at porn is because I don't want to feel the separation from Jesus, not just because 'it's bad.' Also, I was able to address root issues of abandonment with my dad and sexual abuse as a child. I have experienced healing in these areas and forgiveness for those people because of Jesus working through the men and materials in group."

"Before 423, I had no intimate/close relationship with any other guys. Now I have several. I can cry, laugh, share life with other men. Also, I have learned how to have a close, loving intimate (sexually, emotionally, etc.) relationship with my wife. Complete night and day difference in this category for me since joining the group."

Pursuit of Porneia

Dave Scriven

DEDICATION

To Adonica who encouraged, cajoled, challenged, and inspired me to be a better man every single day of our twenty-one and one half years together.

TABLE OF CONTENTS

Preface

Early Wednesday morning, April 27th, 2016

She is the love of my life. I have not seen her for a long while, and I deeply miss her. But she is here now, waiting for me with the same famous, gorgeous smile that had smitten me the first day I saw her over twenty years ago. She looks up at me with love and devotion, just like she did during courtship and each year of our glorious marriage. I cannot contain my joy. Adonica is back! No words can describe my relief. "I thought you were gone," I whisper. She is beautiful, just as I remember her. Short silver hair, trendy glasses, soft and warm petite body, conservative attire, and fluttering eyes silently communicating sincere affection. We hug for what feels like the first time in a very long time. I glance behind her into the bedroom. She had candles lit in preparation for our night of romance.

The last thing I remember before I awake from my incredible dream is the notion that I have finally found what was lost. I am ecstatic, until I remember where I am. Alone in my bed and without the love of my life.

Inspiration for this book flows from the sacred memory of my best friend and dear wife of twenty years. Adonica died of Acute Myeloid Leukemia (AML) on August 30th, 2015 just a few days before her 51st birthday. She bravely battled her disease for ten months before succumbing. Adonica was not afraid to die. Her confidence in God's plan was unshakable. It saddened her, however, when she thought of the pain her departure would cause our children and me. About two weeks before she took her last breath, Adonica softly wept, "My suffering may have an endpoint soon, but the rest of my family, their suffering is going to be much longer. That's painful for me."

I'm still in love with this woman. I suspect I always shall be.

Adonica was an enthusiastic and unwavering supporter of 423 Men which takes its title from Proverbs 4.23 (NIV, NAS).

"Guard your heart with all diligence,
for from it flow the springs of life."

This Adonica did well.

If I am qualified to write this book, it is only because of my own sexual brokenness. I was stuck for thirty-five years in the cycle of shame. I lost my first marriage, my ministry as a Presbyterian clergyman, and my sense of self. While sexually addictive behavior was not the primary reason for these losses, it certainly played a contributing role.

I was saved from the ravages of this terrible addiction starting in 1998 through help I received in For Men Only (FMO), a sexual recovery program of Pure Desire Ministries founded in 1994 by Dr. Ted Roberts. I am forever grateful for this mentor and man of God. Two critical truths emerged during the early years of my recovery:

1. I could stop bad sexual behavior, but I could not do it alone.

2. My addictive sexual behavior pattern was not all about sex.

The latter point prompted me to ask the all-important question, "Why?" If my sexual misbehavior was not about sex, why then did I do it? My personal journey of self-discovery revealed answers that both terrorized me and filled me with wonder and hope. This book is for everyone who has ever repeatedly tried and failed to overcome this destructive addiction, as I did for over three decades. If *I* can get better, *anybody* can.

My friend, Dr. Debi Miller, posed an interesting idea to me recently. "I think this program [423 Men] could be replicated for multiple settings… Aren't we all in a sense addicted to sin? We ALL need life change. We are all in bondage to behaviors rooted in coping mechanisms we've developed as an alternative to confession and repentance." I think Dr. Miller is right. We are "all in a sense addicted to sin," and the principles contained in this book may well apply to recovery from other types of addictions.

My particular sin, addiction, and form of bondage was rooted in "the pursuit of porneia," so I have limited my content primarily to a discussion of a way out of the nightmare called sex addiction. Whether or not the concepts in the pages to follow apply to recovery from other addictive behaviors is a determination better made by readers than by me. I can only speak for myself; about my history of sexual misconduct and the ministry God has graciously allowed and equipped me to perform.

I am Ebenezer Scrooge. I woke up from a bad dream and was given a second chance at life.

Dave Scriven
August 30th, 2016

Held hostage by shame
Deception strangles my soul
How long 'til I'm free?

Haiku Poem by Keith Ervin

Wretched man that I am!

Who will set me free from the body of this death?

Thanks be to God through Jesus Christ our Lord!

The Apostle Paul

Romans 7.24-25a NAS

1 THE JOURNEY OF SELF-DISCOVERY

423 Men is not about stopping your bad sexual behavior. It is about discovering the reasons for your bad sexual behavior. You made the decision to enter a recovery program like 423 Men because you are fed up with your never-ending pursuit of πορνεία[1] and you are ready to make a change. You hope 423 Men will do for you what you cannot do for yourself. You think the program will make you stop misbehaving sexually. It never happens, at least not in the way you expect.

Perhaps you got caught using online pornography at work by the PR Department of your company, or your wife discovered a record of seductive texts with another woman on your cell phone, or the judge threatened jail time for your crime of patronizing a prostitute, or the pastor delivered a stirring sermon on the subject of purity last Sunday and you 'feel convicted.' You may be prompted,

---

[1] Πορνεία is an ancient Greek word found in the biblical manuscripts. It may be pronounced por-NAY-uh and transliterated in English as "porneia." The word is found 25 times in the Greek New Testament and 17 times in the Septuagint (LXX), the Greek translation of the Hebrew Scriptures. It means unlawful sexual intercourse and translated as fornication, sexual immorality, promiscuity, marital unfaithfulness, and loss of virtue. It is sometimes used in the Bible metaphorically pertaining to the practice of idol worship. Dietrich Bonhoeffer described πορνεία as "any sexual irregularity inside or outside of the married life. Such irregularity is sin…" (*The Cost of Discipleship,* chapter 10 "Woman," Simon & Schuster, 1959, p. 133). For the purposes of this book, I will refer to πορνεία as any form or wrong sexual behavior.

by any of a variety of similar circumstances, to get help and to become determined, once and for all, to "Flee πορνεία" (1st Corinthians 6.18a).

What makes this event different than all the other times you got caught or felt convicted, and supposedly became determined to change? The difference is that now, whether persuaded by others or as a matter of personal conscience, you chose to join a community of recovery. Now there is a microscopically thin ray of real hope.

You can overcome sexual sin, but you cannot do it alone. That is not to say that the other guys in your recovery group will become responsible for your healing. No one can make you get better. Jesus will not force you to take the steps necessary to overcome your pattern of sexual sin. Neither will your brothers in recovery. This is one of the hardest lessons, for both addicts and those who love addicts, to learn: No one can make you give up your addiction or bad sex habits; you must do that on your own. Others may cheer you on, but you recover for yourself and by yourself.

True recovery only happens, if it does, in community, but the decision to get better is an individual decision, belonging to you alone. Even if your wife, employer, a court of law, the pastor of your church, or God Himself threatens, "Get treatment, or *else,*" still you find recovery (if you do) and get better (if you do) of your own accord. You cannot fix your problem alone, but neither can anyone else fix it for you.

Herein lies the mystery of redemption every addict longs for: You need a community of support if there is to be even the slightest hope for recovery, but that hope is found within yourself and nowhere else.

Are you that man? If so, you may be blind to "the hope that is [already] in you" (1st Peter 3.15 NAS) until your brothers shine the searchlight of Christ's immeasurable love into the dark and secret regions of your soul. You need your brothers in recovery. They relentlessly remind you that you are fully loved (as you are) and have everything it takes (within yourself) to win your battle against the spirit of πορνεία. You cannot heal alone, but you can heal. You must come out of isolation and join other men in your battle for purity.

A typical guy joining 423 Men expects to hear more of what

he's always heard; that is, to be told by people he deems more capable, powerful, wise, and godly than himself to, "Just stop it." The new member is baffled, early in his recovery, when no one there tells him what to do or stop doing.

As earlier stated, 423 Men is not about stopping a man's bad sexual behavior. It is about discovering the reasons for his bad sexual behavior. The intended byproduct of 423 Men is sexual sobriety, but that is not the focus of recovery. The program is designed, rather, to help each member find out who he is and why he does what he does. Many men in the program find sexual freedom, some for the first time since preadolescence when they first started experimenting with sex, before their activities grew into full-fledged addictive patterns of relapse. Most 423 members are desperate to quit their bad-sex addiction, and have finally arrived at a place where they recognize their need for help. This realization makes them pliable and teachable, which is a great starting point for change, but 423 leaders do not carry a hammer of shame to pound errant brothers into submission.

The new 423 member has grown accustomed to shame. Like a dumb puppy who cannot stop chewing slippers, peeing in the house, barking at nothing, or biting the neighbor's kid, he is a sorry-eyed "bad boy." He's worse than a puppy, because his behavior is no longer cute, experimental, and innocent. He is a full-grown ugly mongrel, utterly incapable of change no matter how many times you smack him with the rolled up newspaper of shame. His pathetic plight is made much worse by virtue of his profession of faith because, while "knowing our Lord and Savior Jesus Christ," he still gets "tangled up and enslaved by sin again" and again and again. He cannot help himself. He is a very bad boy; a dirty dog returning to the smell and taste his own vomit:

> *"With an appeal to twisted sexual desires, they lure back into sin those who have barely escaped from a lifestyle of deception. They promise freedom, but they themselves are slaves of sin and corruption. For you are a slave to whatever controls you. And when people escape from the wickedness of the world by knowing our Lord and Savior Jesus Christ and then get tangled up and enslaved by sin again, they are worse off than before. It would be better if they had never known the way to*

righteousness than to know it and then reject the command they were given to live a holy life. They prove the truth of this proverb: 'A dog returns to its vomit.'" 2nd Peter 2.18-22 NLT

There is a way out of sexual addiction, but more shame will not do the trick. New members may feel as though they deserve a pummeling in 423 Men, but are soon amazed and relieved to learn that, like "wise men from the east" following their encounter with Jesus, they must return home by "another way" (Matthew 2.1, 12 ESV). Loading up with shame never worked before, so why would it work now?

"There is therefore now no condemnation for those who are in Christ Jesus" (Romans 8.1 ESV). Condemnation, denunciation, disapproval, blame, criticism, censure, disgrace, dishonor, discredit, negative remarks, head shaking, and tsk tsk-ing are simply not effective techniques for lasting and positive impact. The addict has already received enough shame, from himself and others. It's time for a change, a real change. If a man is to replace his pursuit of πορνεία with a new passion for the person and work of Jesus Christ, then he must trust Him for "another way," a way that actually works.

The journey of self-discovery works. We've seen it work over and over and over again.

The Journey

Your journey of self-discovery begins with the quest to know yourself; who you are and why you do what you do. It can be a frightening trip and a wild ride, but worth every risk inherent in your decision to embark. Admittedly, you cannot fully know yourself, for today you "see things imperfectly as in a cloudy mirror," but someday you shall "see everything [including yourself] with perfect clarity... just as God now knows [you] completely" (1st Corinthians 13.12 NLT). God knows you better than you know yourself, so you must apply diligence in your pursuit of Him who is able to grant the self-awareness you need for the healing you seek.

You chase after moral purity, then, for yourself and for God, not for others. Healthy sexuality is a personal objective. You are not in recovery to save your marriage, win back your girlfriend, keep your job, or make amends of any kind. It may be too late for that, but have hope. Jesus can fix your personal brokenness and mend the havoc wreaked by sexual addiction. He alone is able to reveal your true self. He will show you the path to the person you were destined to be. Jesus alone can make up for lost time and lost love.

"I will give you back what you lost in the years when swarms of locusts ate your crops." Joel 2.25 TEV

We are on the journey of self-discovery for one purpose: to please God. Pleasing God is our only objective. We have no other agenda. "We make it our aim to please him," (2nd Corinthians 5.9 ESV). We trust Jesus at every step of the journey because trusting God's Son is the only way we can please God. That's it. Nothing more. Nothing less.

"And without trusting, it is impossible to be well pleasing to God." Hebrews 11.6 CJB

The journey of self-discovery is a big, scary adventure. Learning about yourself and why you behave the way you do can be terrifying because of the change self-knowledge demands. Change takes you out of your comfort zone, leads you to places unknown, and threatens much of what you have grown to believe is true about yourself and the world around you. Yet, without personal change, recovery from addiction cannot occur. The path of healing is the path of change, and the journey is not for the timid or the proud. Recovery takes courage and humility and a lot of work, hard work. You can get there, but not alone. You need others to help you.

Near the end of her life, my wife's cancerous white blood cells spiked to their highest levels since her initial diagnosis nine months earlier. Our oncologist recommended we stop chemotherapy, explaining it would not halt the advance of the cancer. Our highly competent and kindhearted Dr. Boriboonsomsin gave us the difficult news that Adonica would only survive a few more weeks. I begged her to keep trying. "There must be something we can do. More chemo, radiation, a new diet, clinical trials, something, anything, please... *please*..." Adonica and Dr. B shook their heads slowly and leaned in close to me. "There's nothing more we can do, Dave. She's ready," whispered Dr. B. Then it was my wife's turn. "I'm tired, Dave. I can't go on like this. You have to let me go now." I became suddenly aware that I, not Adonica, was the reason for this doctor's appointment. Dr. B. and Adonica shared a common, humane mission to help me accept reality, something I have never been very good at. I learned the decision to die was not mine to make. It was hers. I felt helpless, pushed into a corner of acceptance I wasn't ready for. I had to let her go. The abruptness of this realization pierced me at heretofore unknown depths of sorrow. Briefly, I was unable to breathe, then I erupted in tears. I was forced to face the moment I had worked so hard to avoid over the previous two hundred and seventy days of caretaking. We all wept, the three of us, together in Dr. B.'s little medical office.

This unhappy prediction prompted our family to help Adonica achieve a few remaining items on her 'bucket list' which, not surprisingly, included only final activities which our youngest children wished to experience with her.

Our 13-year old daughter, Rachel, wanted to eat frozen yogurt with Mom at Menchie's. Done.

Robert, sixteen, had a higher ambition for his mother. He asked for one final hike with Adonica who, of course, was in no condition to walk to the mailbox, much less a 1½ mile slog to Mirror Lake. Cancer and chemo treatments had ravaged her poor little body but, although she had no strength to climb, she would not be dissuaded. Together with Robert and Rachel, plus four grown stepchildren, four grandkids, and me, Adonica made her way up the mountainside. She ambled a bit, rested a lot, and repeated as necessary, until, near the top, she came to the absolute end of her physical capability. Adonica was literally dying, and could not take another step. The older kids begged her to stop. They could not bear to watch Mom suffer. Robert was noticeably disappointed, but supported his older siblings. I held to the minority opinion and kept pushing Adonica to try harder, until even I caved under the weight of family opinion. Deep lines of sorrow and defeat etched themselves in my wife's face. It was over, and we all knew it. The moment was incredibly disheartening and felt like a cruel end to our loving gesture.

Then someone suggested, "We could carry Mom."

The last ascent was steep and, and fortunately for the burden-bearers in our group, Adonica had lost a lot of weight. The boys and

I took turns successfully packing her tiny 107-pound frame to our intended destination. With our help, and to Robert's great joy, Adonica made it to Mirror Lake one last time. We shall cherish this memory for the rest of our lives.

The journey of self-discovery is painful. Prepare to suffer, but remain steadfast. The upward trek on the mountain of purity is worth every hard-earned and tough-fought stride you take along the way. In the words of Churchill, "Never, never, never give up," even when you stumble and cannot possibly take another step. In your saddest, darkest, most defeated moments, depend on Jesus and your brothers in recovery. Together, you will reach the summit. They may need to carry you, but you will make it to the top. There you will see yourself as you really are... entirely broken and yet fully loved by your Creator and those He called to walk with you.

You are never alone.

Ask "Why?"

The most common misconception about addiction is the reason for it. Consider, for example, sex, gambling, and alcohol addictions:

"Why did he hire a prostitute?"
"Why did she gamble her life's savings?"
"Why did he drive drunk?"

"Why?" is the right question, but the answer is not easily forthcoming. The sex addict did not destroy his family because he wanted to try out sex with a prostitute. The gambling addict did not throw away her children's college fund because she enjoys gambling. The alcoholic did not murder a pedestrian because he likes to drink. Simplistic answers lead to simplistic solutions like, "Stop drinking, gambling, and having sex with prostitutes." This may surprise you, but the addict already thought of that.[2] Simple solutions simply don't work. They don't work because they don't address the reasons for addictive behaviors; the underlying negative

---

[2] For a hilarious parody on this simplistic approach to counseling find Bob Newhart's comedy sketch "Stop It" on YouTube from an old episode of Mad TV where he counsels a woman afraid of being "buried alive in a box."

emotions, the stress points, the broken relationships, the childhood traumas, the internal conflicts, the betrayal, loss, disappointment, or chaos which reside in the addict's soul.

When simple answers fail, as they are bound to, well-intended advice-givers may feel offended, indignant, even judgmental. Compassion goes out the window and onlookers smugly adopt the notion that the addict got the grief he deserved because he refused to heed their sound (and simplistic) advice. Those who intend to help without the knowledge to do so, soothe themselves with the uninformed (and arrogant) premise, "I tried to tell him the truth, but he's too stubborn (and stupid) to listen."

Most addicts I have met are people of integrity. They know and want to do the right thing. So, why would a man with integrity do what he knows is wrong? The answer is, he wouldn't, unless he was addicted. There is a demonic stronghold in the addict's life. It is not possible for him to "just say no" to his drug of choice. Why does a man of God commit a sexual sin when he knows it is morally wrong? Is it because he likes sex? No. We all like sex, but that is not the reason he gets in bed with πορνεία. The addict pursues his sex drug because he cannot NOT pursue it. He is an addict, who must now embark on the journey of self-discovery. He must find the real reasons for his addictive behavior.

The entry point into the 423 Men recovery program is an intake interview. We do not allow men to attend trial group meetings to determine for themselves if 423 is a good fit. We conduct a thirty minute intake interview to help manage a man's expectations about group. This policy is designed to protect the anonymity and confidentiality of all 423 members. The interviewee is fully informed of the 423 Men process and given an opportunity to ask questions. He authorizes an application and a confidentiality agreement. The prospective member decides to join 423 Men, or not, at the intake interview before attending his first group meeting.

I have conducted intakes with well over eight hundred candidates for 423 membership during the past nine and half years. At the initial interview, I explain the cycle of shame outlined in the next chapter and ask each man exactly the same question: "Do you personally relate to the repeating pattern of emotional pain, addictive behavior, and shame?" The answer is always affirmative.

Most nod in hearty agreement, as if to suggest, "Of course I do. Doesn't everyone?" Unless he is in utter denial, the typical guy addicted to sex easily grasps the idea that sex is a process drug he uses to medicate the pain of underlying negative emotions. Unfortunately, knowing the truth and living it are not the same thing. Before any man can live a moral life consistent with his convictions, he must seek to discover why he repeatedly chooses to do something different. He must learn for himself why he would sin sexually rather than trust Jesus. The path of recovery is the path of self-discovery. If recovery is to work, it must first address the reasons for a guy's misbehavior. The journey, then, begins with the question "Why?" Every addict who intends to get better must ask himself, "Why do I act out sexually?"

"Why?" is the all-important inquiry, holding the key to our recovery. The question is simple enough, but the answer is anything but simple, and may take years to uncover. As Ted Roberts states in his seminal work on breaking the bonds of sexual addiction, "…our goal is getting healthy, not just stopping destructive behavior. And that will probably take three to five years, with the Holy Spirit doing miracles all along the way, as you cooperate."[3] Dr. Roberts further draws from his own experience, "My battle with sexual bondage wasn't… simple. I went through nearly three and a half years of absolute war before I could see any daylight on the issue."[4] Recovery takes time, and it starts with the question, "Why?"

Oscar Wilde amusingly observed, "I can resist anything except temptation."[5] Most addicts feel the same, but they must learn to resist the lure of bad sex, at least for a few seconds, in order to ask themselves the critical question. When contemplating sin like internet porn use, masturbation with sexual fantasies, or objectifying a young woman by mentally undressing her, a man in active recovery will stop just long enough to inquire, "Why am I doing this?" Even if he chooses to sin, he made a bit of progress worth celebrating in that rare time of honest self-reflection. 423 Men teaches progress, not perfection. Two steps forward and one step

---

[3] *Pure Desire*, Ted Roberts, Revised & Updated, Regal, 2nd Edition, 2008, p. 75.
[4] Ibid, p. 85.
[5] From Oscar Wilde's 1892 comedy in four acts entitled "Lady Windermere's Fan, A Play About a Good Woman."

back is still progress.

As a man engages the practice of asking "Why?" he may eventually pose to himself further questions the "Why?" question begs:

"What negative feelings am I trying to medicate with this addictive behavior?"

"Am I feeling sad, angry, lonely, bored, scared, hurt, disillusioned, stressed, or something else?"

"Why am I feeling sad, angry, lonely, bored, scared, hurt, disillusioned, stressed, or something else?"

"What responsible action could I possibly take to resolve the cause of my negative emotions?"

Why Ask "Why"?

Asking the "Why?" question is beneficial in two ways. First, this self-reflective process slows the addict down. It may even interrupt the addictive cycle long enough for the man to gather his mental faculties as the intensity of the temptation lessens. If he comes to his senses during a moment of thoughtful self-probing, the addict earns a small victory which he can file away and later report to his brothers at the next 423 Men meeting. There he may be greeted with applause and high fives. A win like this is empowering and provides a foundation of success the recovering addict can build upon.

Secondly, the guy gets to know himself. There is no better time than just prior to engaging in the addictive behavior to delve deeply into an exploration of self. When every part of a man's being cries out for his sex drug, a little self-denial will force him to feel the pain of withdrawal. This crisis becomes the perfect occasion for the addict to start the investigative process of discovering the personal issues which historically have been the driving force behind his addiction. This approach is the addict's version of the biblical mandate, "Resist the devil and he will flee from you. Draw near to

God and He will draw near to you" (James 4.7-8a NAS). Unpleasant feelings exist for a reason, and it's the addict's job in recovery to find out why they exist. "What am I feeling right now?" and "Why do I feel the way I do?" and finally, "What can I do about it?"

As the addict confronts himself and his feelings, prayer becomes his best friend. One of the most effective is the "Serenity Prayer" in conjunction with personalized lines from the "Lord's Prayer" and guidance from Apostle Paul.

"God grant me the serenity
To accept the things I cannot change;
Courage to change the things I can;
And the wisdom to know the difference. [6]

"And lead me not into temptation, but deliver me from evil."

"No temptation has overtaken me except what is common to mankind. And God is faithful; he will not let me be tempted beyond what I can bear. But when I am tempted, he will provide a way out so that I can endure it."[7]

This process of self-analysis is not intuitive. It's much easier to run into the comforting embrace of our beloved πορνεία, but godly resistance is not futile. The Bible says, "Flee πορνεία" (1st Corinthians 6.18a). It can be done. Your recovery plan works, if you work the plan. It takes prayer, practice, patience, perseverance, and most importantly, time spent each week with supportive brothers in recovery who are on their own journeys of self-discovery with you.

There is Hope

Success in any endeavor depends on hope. We possess an astounding capacity for longsuffering in difficult situations as long

---

[6] Attributed to American theologian, Reinhold Niebuhr, published in 1951 and adopted by Alcoholics Anonymous and other 12-Step recovery programs.
[7] Adapted from the words of Jesus in His famous 'Sermon on the Mount' recorded by gospel writer Matthew (6.13 KJV) and Paul in his first letter to the Corinthian church (10.13 NIV 2011).

as hope is alive. But when the flame dims and hope is extinguished, it's all over. We engage in a process of slow death by grasping at habit-forming activities, like πορνεία, and their false promise of a life with meaning. We want the truth that *"will set you free"* (John 8.32) but instead, we settle for a B.T.N. (better than nothing), lesser truth. It's a counterfeit replica of truth, but it's all (we think) we have. Our bad situations worsen as misguided and addictive actions escalate in the desperate search for hope in all the wrong places.

Many nine-to-fivers live for the weekend in hope of filling the space of forty-eight hours with enough television, recreation, sex, food, sleep, and alcohol to sustain them for another five days of drudgery at meaningless jobs. The overachiever falls into exactly the same trap. As a successful professional, he gropes for the illusion of significance and trades his family and faith for a career promising status, peer approval, and the finer things only high salaries can provide. But hope is not a commodity. It cannot be bought even with hyper-dedication to a temporal goal.

Hope begins at a particular point… the point of *truth*. It's more than theological truth. It's the truth about *you*… your calling, your God-given design, your relationship with Jesus, your purpose, your dreams, your 'who-I-am-ness.' You must be clear, very clear on this truth. Know Him and know yourself. This is your journey of self-discovery. Don't sell out for a smaller truth or another person's truth. Find the truth about you. Keep searching until you peel away every layer of false hope and discover the real, naked, and unencumbered you. Jesus will meet you there. He'll take you by the hand and show you the inner worlds you must conquer. He'll reveal your original destiny. He'll impart a single-minded focus-ability empowering you to drive with all your might "toward the goal for the prize of the upward call of God in Christ Jesus" (Philippians 3.14). This is your truth and it's the only place to find lasting hope. This is the hope worth living for because it's based on a truth worth dying for.

Once you get this hope, never let it go. Keep hope alive "through perseverance and the encouragement of the Scriptures," as Paul exhorted the church in Rome:

"For whatever was written in earlier times was written for our instruction, that through perseverance and the encouragement of the Scriptures we might have hope." Romans 15.4 NASB

Recovery is not about stopping your bad sexual behavior. It is about discovering the reasons for your bad sexual behavior. It's about knowing who you are and why you do what you do. You can climb the mountain of self-discovery and there find the purity and freedom you seek. With help from Jesus and your brothers in recovery, you will reach the summit. Never give up hope. Have hope in the never-ending love and redemptive power of Jesus which purifies you, just as He Himself is pure.

"We know that when He appears, we will be like Him, because we will see Him as He is. And everyone who has this hope in Him purifies himself just as He is pure." 1st John 3.2b-3 HCSB

There is hope.

2 THE CYCLE OF SHAME

Pain

It's a dirty, four-letter word... P – A – I – N. We all carry some of it, at our core.

I enjoy racquetball and have played since I took *Racquetball* as an elective class at the University of Washington over forty-five years ago. Today I cannot participate in this sport without pain. I still play singles religiously three times a week, and live on vitamin "I" (Ibuprofen), physical therapy, and ice. I am determined to stay in good physical shape and I love to compete, but there's a price to pay. The price is pain.

Pain is a reality, especially for aging people who are active, but there is a form of suffering as bad as, or even worse than, physical pain, and that is emotional pain. Loneliness, confusion, fear, depression, anxiety, stress, worry, panic, feelings of inadequacy and self-doubt, hopelessness, despair, boredom, unresolved conflicts, childhood traumas, and a host of other underlying negative emotions seem to define our human condition. None of us are immune from inner pain, even those who appear on the outside as 'having it all together.' Help is available but most of us are too proud or embarrassed to ask for it. Instead, we pretend all is well and choose to live with turmoil brewing just beneath the surface of a calm exterior. We are nothing more, and perhaps much less, than the image we try to portray.

Try this magic trick the next time you are speaking with a group of young men. Tell them you will predict their next word and write 'good' on a piece of paper. Fold the paper and offhandedly ask one of them, "Hey, how are you?" Catch him by surprise and he will invariably answer, "Good." Open your folded page and reveal to the group the same word on your scrap of paper. It's a funny gimmick when it works, and it usually does. You don't have to be a psychic, mind-reader, or prophet to know that people will almost always respond in the affirmative. (Use the word "Fine" if performing this trick with an older crowd.)

When a man says he's "good," that's usually code for "I'm strong. I am a rock. I have no problems. I'm Superman. I am invincible, invulnerable, capable, and without weakness. I have muscles. I am an island. I'm a stud." If the typical man cannot freely and easily share inner feelings, it may be due to his fear of exposing weakness, a self-preservation instinct which, of course, betrays a form of weakness in itself.

It's impossible to avoid pain. If you are in distress, then welcome to the human race. If you are not now suffering in some way, enjoy the reprieve, but get ready because it's coming. It's a good life, but never perfect. Pain is real and will show up when you least want or expect it. The happy face I wear to appear professional or spare others can, at times, be nothing more than a mask to cover the agony of my aching soul.

Many adults cannot identify the source, or even the existence, of emotional pain. It may be chronic instead of acute, flying just below the radar and avoiding detection by self and others. They recall their early years as idyllic and uneventful, but I'm not always persuaded by those who claim, "I had a great childhood." Every child's needs are unique and no parent is perfectly suited to meet all of them. It is impossible to fully protect young people from the pitfalls and woundedness typical of the growing up years. Kids get lost in the social shuffle, shrink under the pressures of family dysfunction, and hide from contact with the outer world. Envision the teen boy draped in an oversized hoody, eyes covered by long hair, and ears plugged with music. His body language is easy to read. He wants nothing to do with you. A host of adolescent apprehensions are fueling these early patterns of isolation and secrecy. Self-protective habits evolve and rituals of comfort get reenacted many times over. Will he outgrow his withdrawn-ness and mistrust of the outside world? Maybe not. In due course, he may learn to portray an attractive persona and adopt a more sophisticated wall of protection, one that is harder to detect, but present nonetheless.

We all carry emotional pain. As noted, we hurt because we are human. Pain transcends time, space, gender, age, class, culture, and national origin. None of us escape the scathing effects of betrayal, loss, disappointment, and grief. It's part of our humanness and this thing we call life. You will experience a gamut of emotional ups and downs throughout your years on earth: love, surprise, joy, fear, and sorrow. You will laugh, cry, hurt, suffer, and hope. You'll often demonstrate a healthy and sturdy outer appearance, but may be broken and wounded within. I suspect every human, in moments of honesty, would admit, "Handle me with care. I am fragile." Given the wrong set of circumstances, like the loss of a job, a car wreck, a messy divorce, or even a harsh word, and anyone can break, sometimes beyond emotional repair.

Emotional pain is the door by which addictions access our sore and tender souls.

Addiction

"Addiction" comes from the Latin word *addictus* meaning "to yield; give assent, sell" or figuratively, "to devote or sell out." Its etymology points to two original Latin words: *ad* (to) and *dicere* (say, declare). Those who display addictive behaviors are declaring their allegiance to an activity which ultimately takes control of their lives. Addictions are described in various translations of ancient biblical literature as "strongholds," "powers," "fortresses," "the thief," "principalities," "cosmic powers," "world forces of this darkness," "evil rulers and authorities of the unseen world," and "spiritual wickedness in high places" (see John 10.10; Romans 8.38; 2nd Corinthians 10.4; Ephesians 6.12). Addictions are destructive. They represent a supernatural power capable of squeezing every vestige of life from those who yield to their dark influence. Jesus said, "The thief comes only to steal and kill and destroy," (John 10.10 NIV). Addictions destroy hope, life, and destiny. Addictions are demonic in their source and intent.

There are two kinds of addictions. *Chemical* addictions begin with the practice of ingesting a substance like cocaine, nicotine, alcohol, methamphetamine, or heroin. A *process* addiction is characterized by extreme devotion to activities like gambling, sex, work, shopping, video games, or even unnatural attachments to other people or causes. Those who study brain functions say the effect of chemical and process addictions are similar. Both release a naturally occurring chemical called dopamine into the pleasure center of the user's brain. Herein lies the value of addictions to the addict. They take away pain.

The amazing and terrible truth about addictions is... they *work!* No one would use drugs if they did not possess some seemingly positive and immediate benefits. Process and chemical drug abuse anesthetizes, medicates, and softens the negative realities of our existence. They 'take the edge off' emotional pain. If we start from the premise that all people carry some level of internal pain, then it is easy to understand the theoretical reason behind addiction. Of course, it is monumentally difficult for most people to admit they have addictive tendencies, much less adopt for themselves the "addict" label. Even those in active recovery find it extraordinarily challenging to make the connection between the pain caused by their own unresolved issues and the pattern of their addictive lifestyles. Denial plays a huge role in the addict's thought process. What we may understand conceptually, or see so readily in others, is almost impossible to recognize in ourselves.

Consider, for example, the husband and wife having an argument. They are suffering from long-term and intense marital discord. Like so many spats in the past, they cannot achieve resolution. The couple parts in a huff and, without thinking, both go immediately to their drug of choice. The husband looks at online pornography and the wife heads for the refrigerator. Why? No conscious choices are made. Rather, without thinking they each find comfort in decades-old habits of seeking immediate solace for their wounded souls. Instead of making the courageous decision to seek help and fix the marriage, they migrate toward what they know works to mitigate their suffering right now.

People who exhibit addictive behavior patterns are not bad people. They are hurting people with the buildup of layers of emotional pain; in some cases, dating back to childhood. When they were too young to know better, they became desperate to find a solution to the traumas that beleaguered their preadolescent souls.

423 Men is an organization dedicated to helping men discover the reasons for, and eventually overcome, their habits of unhealthy sexual practices, like frequenting strip clubs, adult book stores, and nude beaches, engaging in one night stands, sex with prostitutes, co-ed naked hot-tubbing, web cam sex, sexual intercourse outside of marriage, emotional affairs, same sex encounters, and inappropriate flirtation or touching, paying for sexual massages and phone sex, sexting, viewing and sharing media with explicit content, sexualizing and mentally undressing women, allowing uncontrolled lustful thoughts and fantasies, and a myriad of other sexually stimulating activities. The most common addictive practice among the hundreds of men who have participated in 423 Men since its inception in September 2009 is internet pornography and masturbation using sexually arousing images and streaming videos.

My pursuit of πορνεία began when I was in third grade at the age of eight. I thought often of my pretty female classmates and wondered what they might look like without their clothes on. I used tracing paper to draw the outline of women in the underwear section of the Sears and Roebuck catalog. I had seen my mother naked when I was only five, so I had a general recollection of a woman's body parts and used my pencil to fill in the blanks. When I was in fifth grade I hit the jackpot. My dad subscribed to *Playboy* magazine and usually kept a copy hidden under the T-shirts in his closet. Can you guess where I headed every time my parents left me home alone? These personal sexual experiences predated the advent of the Internet by nearly thirty-five years when America Online (AOL) made World Wide Web access an open door for anyone with a dial-up modem and a personal computer.[8] For the past twenty years or more, the Internet has made pornography accessible, affordable, and anonymous ("The Three A's"), but when I was a kid, getting porn was much more challenging. I had to find a magazine for visual

---

[8] America Online was founded in 1985 under the name Quantum Computer Services. The company surpassed 500,000 members in 1993, the same year that its mass disc mailings made AOL a household name. By 1995 AOL had grown to one million members.

sexual stimulation, and became adept at locating printed porn, not only in my dad's closet, but also hidden stashes in my buddies' dads' and older brothers' closets, as well as the local garbage dumps. I was on a mission and found other young friends to join me in my quest for sex.

Sexual curiosity usually begins for boys before puberty. Males start exploring pornography most commonly around the age of ten. The majority of experts agree that the human brain is not fully developed until the mid- or late twenties. During the developmental stage, a boy may secretly and routinely fill his mind with graphic sexual images, especially when faced with difficulties like conflicts with siblings and parents, rejection at school, or failing grades. His brain creates neuropathways which become entrenched as his way of dealing with emotional pain. Should it surprise us when a married man instinctively migrates toward online porn when he gets angry, hurt, lonely, stressed, or bored? Of course not. He's been going there since he was ten years old! His porn habit is not his wife's fault, of course. His sex addiction predates his first encounter with the woman he chose to marry, usually by many years.

The stakes are high. Unchecked, the addictive cycle will progress and destroy all that is good in the lives of hurting people.

Shame

God created us with a beautiful gift called a "conscience," although we do not always heed its warnings. A conscience is designed to impart feelings of guilt when we do something wrong. It follows then, that guilt is also a divine gift reminding us when we miss the mark or behave in an ungodly or immoral way. Guilt allows us to become aware of our need for forgiveness and to hold on to the promise of God: "If we confess our sins, [God] is faithful and just and will forgive us our sins and purify us from all unrighteousness," (1st John 1.9 NIV).

The addict has a hard time with forgiveness. He cannot easily forgive himself. As an addict I have often told myself, "What the heck. I've gone this far, I might as well go all the way." This rationale takes a man or woman outside the reach of forgiveness, or so they think. Offenders surrender to the grip of toxic shame and generally consider themselves beyond redemption. This, of course, is not the way of God:

"Like water spilled on the ground, which cannot be recovered, so we must die. But that is not what God desires; rather, he devises ways so that a banished person does not remain banished from him." 2nd Samuel 14.14 NIV 2011

"God... desires all people to be saved and to come to the knowledge of the truth." 1st Timothy 2. 3b-4 ESV

" 'As I live!' declares the Lord GOD, 'I take no pleasure in the death of the wicked, but rather that the wicked turn from his way and live.' " Ezekiel 33.11a NAS

Guilt offers great hope. Shame robs a person of hope. Guilt is about what I do. Shame is about who I am. Guilt tweaks my conscience and reminds me that something wrong needs fixing. Shame is an internal, negative self-assessment convincing me that I am flawed, defective, and beyond help. Shame cripples me. I become, in my own mind, worthless. I loathe myself. If others really knew me, they would also despise and hate me. If they hate me, then it is for good reason because I, too, hate myself. I am intrinsically worthless and because I am not worthy of love or lovable, I must continue to hide and isolate my true identity from the world around me. I am all alone. No one understands. I am the walking dead. So goes the sad, internal process of the addict.

The man trapped in the cycle of shame has a choice, but he doesn't know it. Undoubtedly, the shame he feels adds to and compounds the emotional pain he hoped to deaden by use of his sexual addiction. Now he feels even more pain. The answer? Go back to the addiction for relief from mental anguish. The pain again disappears, of course, but only for a short while. When the shame returns, it does so with an even greater paralyzing force than the time before. A man caught in the web of sexual addiction will find a "hit" from his particular act of πορνεία, but when he is done visiting the strip club, having sex with a prostitute, sexualizing an attractive woman, mentally undressing his neighbor's wife, or masturbating to the erotic idol on his computer screen, his soul is again flooded with shame. This shame is overpowering and cannot be ignored. It must be addressed and relieved. No man can remain standing under the crushing weight of shame's power. Not one. He will always return to the fleeting comfort of his addiction. The addict will repeat the vicious cycle over, and over, and over again until he destroys himself. There is no way out. Alone, the addict will die in his sin.

Even shame, as destructive as it is, has a redemptive end goal. Shame is a penetrating and final wakeup call. It presents us with a choice. Will we allow crippling shame to bring us to our knees before the ruler of Hell? Or, will we 'come to our senses' and, like the prodigal son in the pigpen of our own making, find our way back to a loving Father (Luke 15.11-32)? To "know... shame" means we are still alive to the possibility of hope, "but the wicked know no shame" (Zephaniah 3.5 NLT). We must not let shame have its way with us, but rather recognize it for what it is: a warning sign directing us to run back to God and our brothers in recovery before it's too late. The road to healing is never easy, but if we take the first step, we will find others to help us along the way. We can overcome sexual sin, but we cannot do it alone.

Biblical Case Study

In the story of Jesus we read about two men who turned their backs on Jesus. There was no essential difference between the actions of Peter and Judas. Both betrayed Jesus, one by refusing to acknowledge his association with the Rabbi, and the other by revealing Jesus' whereabouts. Peter was wracked with guilt, "wept bitterly," and eventually became the leader of the early church. Judas was "seized with remorse" and shame, returned his "blood money," then "hanged himself" (see Matthew 26.75; 27.3-5). The real difference between these two disciples lies in the distinction between guilt and shame. Peter felt guilty. Judas was filled with shame.

Failure is everyone's story. Peter failed and Judas failed. You and I also fail, routinely. Peter sought forgiveness. Judas killed himself. Peter's guilt led him to repentance. Judas' shame led to self-destruction. Peter recognized his need for a Savior. Judas assumed he was beyond redemption and, like a sheep led to slaughter, cooperated with Satan's plan for his life – permanent and total destruction. Peter found hope and redemption. Judas lost hope and was hopelessly lost.

Do we believe the lie that our betrayal of Jesus with the sin of πορνεία pushes us beyond the outer limits of the forgiveness He freely offers? We may understand Christ's substitutionary atonement at an intellectual level, but has the truth of salvation seeped down into our souls? Has the light of God's forgiveness penetrated every corner of our inner darkness? Will we, like Judas, "end up on a deathbed of regrets" (2nd Corinthians 7.10 *The Message*)?

Two qualities characterize a person in recovery… courage and humility. "God is opposed to the proud, but gives grace to the humble" (James 4.6 NAS, quoting Proverbs 3.34). Like the men in 423 Men, Peter was humble and courageous. Judas, on the other hand, was a proud coward.

- Pride: If Judas couldn't redeem himself, then no one could, not even Jesus.

- Cowardice: Judas could not bear to face his brokenness and chose to end his life, which, of course, is the grand objective of all addictions.

Peter "broke down" and "wept bitterly" (Mark 14.72; Matthew 26.75 NIV) at the painful realization that, when his faith was on the line, he did not measure up to his promise of loyalty he made to Jesus. When Peter proved to himself that he was a loser, it would have been easy for him to follow the example of Judas and consider himself beyond the reach of redemption.

Peter did not quit, in spite of the intensity of the emotional pain. Instead, the fallen disciple mustered the *courage* to feel the depth of his depravity and gathered the *humility* to admit his pitiful condition. Peter's "Godly sorrow" drove him into the arms of a loving Savior and an active community of faith.

"Godly sorrow brings repentance that leads to salvation and leaves no regret, but worldly sorrow brings death."
2nd Corinthians 7.10 NIV

Continuing down the road of addiction guarantees our eventual demise. Most addicts are not suicidal, but the practice of addiction is a form of slow suicide, because, after the novelty wears off, continued drug use evolves into a form of self-punishment the addict can no longer cease to inflict. He is following the path of Judas and may not even know it until it's too late. The distinction between Judas and Peter, shame and guilt, is more subtle than the addict surmises.

Ending the cycle of shame is painful. Prepare to suffer. The spirit of πορνεία will not yield without a fight. Saying "no" to your sex drug hurts, but it will not kill you. Do not submit with Judas-like resignation to the pathetic path of self-destruction. Rather, surrender your will to the will of Him who alone can impart the grace to endure the pain and "fight the good fight" (1st Timothy 1.18; 6.12 NAS).

We are not Judas. We do not give up on ourselves and, by our very inaction, paint ourselves into the 'corner of last resort' where taking action to end our suffering once and for all becomes the easy, and seemingly only, remedy to our pitiful predicament.

We are Peter. We willingly face and embrace emotional pain, and suffer for as long as we must, while maintaining hope for redemption. We proclaim with Job, "Though He slay me, yet will I trust Him" (Job 13.15 NKJV). We trust Jesus. We do not give up.

Human suffering is inevitable. Redemptive suffering is a choice you make. Prepare to suffer, but suffer with hope. Trust Him who "will make the Valley of Trouble a door of hope" (Hosea 2.15 NCV).

In her 1932 Pulitzer Prize winning book *The Good Earth*, Pearl Buck brilliantly and artfully describes the course of sexual addiction in the life of a peasant farmer around the turn of the last century in China. After enduring unspeakable poverty, Wang Lung finally achieves a measure of success and wealth. He becomes arrogant and loses his moral bearings. Driven by lower instincts he pursues his lust for a young prostitute, learning the hard way that bad sex never satisfies.

"...fevered, filled with a sickened hunger, he followed slavishly, bit by bit, her unfolding, until the moment of crisis, when, like a flower that is ripe for plucking, she was willing that he should grasp her wholly.

"Yet never could he grasp her wholly, and this it was which kept him fevered and thirsty, even if she gave him his will of her. When O-lan [Wang Lung's wife] had come to his house it was health to his flesh and he lusted for her robustly as a beast for its mate and he took her and was satisfied and he forgot her and did his work content. But there was no such content now in his love for this girl, and there was no health in her for him. At night when she would have no more of him, pushing him out of the door petulantly, with her small hands suddenly strong on his shoulders, his silver thrust into her bosom, he went away hungry as he came. It was as though a man, dying of thirst, drank the salt water of the sea which, though it is water, yet dries his blood into thirst and yet greater thirst so that in the end he dies, maddened by his very drinking. He went in to her and he had his will of her again and again and he came away unsatisfied."[9]

Pearl Buck's hero is inexplicably determined to destroy himself. What compels smart people to do stupid things? Ask former New York Governor Eliot Spitzer, or Bill Clinton and Monica Lewinsky, or an Islamic suicide bomber, or a compulsive gambler, or a guy hooked on endless hours of internet porn, or the abused wife returning home for more of the same. There is no answer beyond pointless rhetoric, pathetic excuses, and empty apologies. "Fallen! Fallen is Babylon the Great," but lost and hurting souls still "drink the maddening wine of her adulteries" (Revelation 14.8). Like the Gerasene demoniac, they are "driven by the demon into solitary places" of personal destruction (Luke 8.29 NIV).

The same man who forced a "Legion" of devils into a herd of pigs, offers every hopeless addict "authority over all demons" (Luke 8.30ff; 9.1 KJV). You can overcome sexual sin, but not alone.

There is hope and there is a way out.

---

[9] The Good Earth, Pearl S. Buck, Washington Square Press, 1931, p. 181.

3 RECOVERY MYTHS

Most addicts know they need help but they would rather die than ask for it. Requesting assistance is like asking for directions when we are lost. It is a sign of inadequacy or an admission of weakness, a condition we must hide at all costs. Dependence on anyone other than self is a violation of the entirely unsupportable premise, "If I am broken, I can fix myself." This declaration is not a sign of faith. It's nothing more than an unwarranted act of presumption. The addict's confidence is a pretense for cockiness. He is like the over-zealous and misguided Hebrew warriors who "in their presumption went up" (Numbers 14.44 NIV) to fight the Amalekites without the approval of Moses or the Ark of the Covenant. These proud idealists soon found themselves running for their lives. Self-assured addicts should take a tip from the insanely naïve and ignorant gesture of Skeva's sons, Jewish exorcists who, upon encountering an evil spirit, received "such a beating that they ran from the house, naked and bleeding" (Acts 19.16 CJB). The spirit of πορνεία is nothing to fool with. Do not underestimate the power, experience, or single-minded intent of this fierce supernatural opponent. Only God can take down an enemy of this caliber. Human effort is useless in the battle for sexual purity.

> *"Oh, please help us against our enemies,*
> *for all human help is useless.*
> *With God's help we will do mighty things,*
> *for he will trample down our foes."* Psalm 108.12 – 13 NLT

Self-aggrandized notions of easy remedies devolve into impossible promises never kept. Like Peter's false bravado, "Even if I have to die with you, I will never deny you" (Mark 14.31 *The Message*), the man caught in the cycle of shame will, against all evidence to the contrary, claim he has what it takes to kick the πορνεία habit. He thinks he can stop anytime he wants to. He's wrong, of course. He may not want to admit it, but it is impossible for him to stop. Alone, it cannot be done.

As a young pastor in an unhappy marriage and struggling ministry, I would occasionally feel overcome by lust and purchase a pornographic magazine at the local convenience store. I would actually pray as I entered the mini-mart... pray that the kid behind the counter taking my money was not in my youth group! I pulled a woolen beanie over my head and desperately hoped to keep my identity a secret. I could not afford to be recognized.

Why would I take such a risk? Why did I jeopardize my marriage, ministry, and reputation for a dirty magazine? The answer is simple. I was an addict. I *had* to have my fix, and would do *anything* to get it. When I was done using the publication, that is "spilling my seed" (Genesis 38.9) before colorful pages filled with images of beautiful, young, naked women, I would come partially to my senses and give Jesus assurances I could not possibly honor. "I will never, never, never, never, never, never, NEVER do that again." I made the same promise many times before, but somehow deluded myself into believing this time I meant it. I lived in 'Never, Never, Neverland.' It was a God fantasy which ironically helped to perpetuate my sex fantasy. Promise-making was a critical element in my addictive ritual. The practice made me feel better about my sinful behavior, but was completely disconnected from reality. I was a promise-maker, not a promise-keeper. I thought I could manage my sin by being sincere enough and repenting hard enough, but I was wrong. When it came to my addiction, I was capable of neither sincerity nor repentance.

Most addicts think they can fix themselves but that is a lie. Simple remedies to complex and longstanding addictions are deceptively attractive because they offer the false perception that recovery is quick and easy. Unfortunately, all 'fix-it fallacies' contain elements of truth, making them the worst kind of lies. They allow misguided addicts to hold out for false hope (in some cases, for many years) while they continue full-force in their addictive lifestyle. Recovery is not about believing half-truths as we continue the on-going pursuit of πορνεία, but exposing the lies that have bound us to that pursuit.

How does an addict think he can fix himself? Here is a brief summary of the three most common lies he tells himself with further detail in the sections to follow:

1. "I can do this."

Personal effort *without trust in Jesus* is a form of deception typified by comments (or attitudes) like, "I can fix myself." This is a cover for isolationism and discussed with more detail in the section called "The Myth of Self-Dependency."

2. "I have accountability."

Accountability to others *without real repentance* is a lie commonly hidden behind statements like, "I have some guys who are holding me accountable," and presented in the section entitled "The Myth of People-Dependency."

3. "God will take care of it."

Reliance on God *without obedience to His commands* is one of the worst forms of dishonesty because it sounds so 'spiritual' to say, "God will take care of it." This half-truth is more fully described in the section called "The Myth of God-Dependency."

The Myth of Self-Dependency

Self-dependency is a basic tenet of American culture. "Go west young man," "make something of yourself," "get off your lazy rear end," "get a job," "give it all you got," "be strong," "get your head in the game," "grow up," "act like a man," "man up," etc., and the philosophy embodied in phrases like these, does not work with addiction. Trying harder only brings more heartache and failure. We cannot end the cycle of shame by applying more sweat in our work of recovery. "Do not be deceived" (1st Corinthians 6.9; Galatians 6.7 NAS): we do not control our addiction. It controls us. No amount of good intentions, will power, strength of character, sincerity, positive thinking, positive confession, positivity, or self-confidence will make a difference. Our efforts are futile. We must accept our total and complete powerlessness over "the sin which so easily entangles us" (Hebrews 12.1 NAS).

You cannot trust both Jesus and yourself.

Trusting yourself = not trusting Jesus
Trusting Jesus = not trusting yourself

Our wisdom, our efforts, our energy, our power, and our drive will not get the job done. Our history of failure alone should be enough to prove this point beyond all possible doubt.

Self-reliance is a setup for despair because when it fails, as it inevitably will, we feel hopeless and convince ourselves that nothing, not even Jesus, can save us from our horrid dilemma. We form an unholy alliance with the power of darkness and eventually fully embrace our secret identity. We surrender to biblical anti-truth, becoming "one flesh" with πορνεία (Genesis 2.24) and continue down the path of destruction.

We accept that personal change is "not by [human] might, nor by [personal] power" (Zechariah 4.6 KJV), and therefore conclude change is not possible at all. We become resigned to our shadowy destiny and locked into the false belief that there is no healing for our battered souls. We agree with Scripture's assessment without Scripture's solution. We know from experience that we cannot free ourselves from πορνεία's grip, but we refuse to seek help from our brothers in recovery. So, we continue to lie to ourselves: I can stop sinning sexually. I just have to "try harder," "be more disciplined," "just say 'no' to temptation," and "re-commit myself."

Christian variations of the 'try harder' theme (e.g., read the Bible, pray more fervently, fast weekly, get busy serving God, attend church, sing worship songs, say confessions, witness for Jesus, join a ministry team, pass out Bible tracts, become a missionary, tithe, start a non-profit, etc.) do not guarantee victory over addiction. Trying harder to be good, even after copious amounts of positive self-talk and renewed commitments to change, will not work no matter how well we spin our efforts or how dedicated we try to be.

The foolish confidence of trusting in self will destroy a man, just as both the psalmist and the prophet alleged:

"This is the fate of those who trust in themselves,
and of their followers, who approve their sayings.
They are like sheep and are destined to die;
death will be their shepherd
(but the upright will prevail over them in the morning).

"Their forms will decay in the grave,
far from their princely mansions."
Psalm 49.13-14 NIV 2011

"Because you have depended on your own strength...
all your fortresses will be devastated—"
Hosea 10.13-14 NIV

Personal effort without trust in Someone bigger and higher than ourselves, namely, Jesus Christ and His redemptive power, is a subtle form of pride which paradoxically guarantees our ultimate failure. Check out Proverbs 16.18 in both old and modern English:

"Pride goeth before destruction, and an haughty spirit before a fall." KVJ

"First pride, then the crash —
the bigger the ego, the harder the fall." The Message

The Myth of People-Dependency

Dependency on people holds a two-fold benefit for the addict. At the inception of this form of dependence, the addict has someone who will listen to him, and when it doesn't work, he has someone to blame. Traditional accountability is a form of people-dependency. It will fail because it is based on the premise that confession alone brings healing. True confession is an indispensable first step in our recovery, but that's all it is... a first step only, not the end of the matter. Jesus' younger brother, James, admonished believers, "Confess your trespasses to one another, and pray for one another, that you may be healed" (James 5.16 NKJV). Confession is a critical part of the healing process. Without full disclosure, there can be no victory over sin. We are as sick as our secrets. But confession, even honest confession, does not, in itself, heal us. It is only the starting point.

I was raised as a Roman Catholic and required to "go to confession" every Saturday night with my dad and little brother. I told the priest all the sins I could think of and usually felt better. The practice was cathartic. I was momentarily cleansed and freed from the depravity that plagued my adolescent soul. Hopefully, I would not sin again, at least not before partaking of the Eucharist at Sunday Mass the next morning.

Like the confessional booth, the Protestant version of the Sacrament of Penance assumes truth-telling in an "accountability group" is adequate for long-term change. It is not. I can put a dollar in the communal jar every time I masturbate, snap a rubber band on my wrist whenever I sexualize a young woman, or endure the discomfort of reporting to my accountability partners the truth about my addictive secrets... and still never get better.

This common 'binge and purge' accountability model is flawed and will not provide the help and hope an addict needs. In fact, this accountability practice, left unchecked, can become an acceptable arrangement; an essential element in the ritual of relapse. The man under the spell of πορνεία may wish to feel remorse for his actions and might even work up a few tears, but like Esau who was rejected "even though he sought the blessing with tears" (Hebrews 12.17 NIV 2011) and Orpah who "broke down and cried," but still abandoned her mother-in-law (Ruth 1.9 TLB), the practicing addict becomes adept at putting on a convincing show of repentance for himself and others, but has no intention of change at all.

Heartfelt displays of confession without real repentance undermine the recovery methodology, lulling the user into a comfortable state of counterfeit health. The addict thinks he's okay, but he's not. If the addict can tolerate the belittling and dehumanizing practice of pleading guilty to his disgraceful behavior in group, he may subconsciously believe he has, thereby, paid for his sins. He becomes his own Jesus; his own redeemer. The man in this state will not and cannot change. His weekly routine of so-called "accountability" and embarrassing self-exposure earns him a free pass for another week of sexual misconduct. Yes, he is 'the scum of the earth' and knows it, and his group knows it, but at least he's being "honest" with his accountability group and the bonus is… he gets to continue his dearly beloved addiction.

This ungodly arrangement; that is the acknowledgment of sin without true repentance, is an occasion of great sadness for everyone who truly cares for the addict. The Apostle Paul expressed it as a form of grief:

"And I will be grieved because many of you have not given up your old sins. You have not repented of your impurity, sexual immorality [πορνεία], and eagerness for lustful pleasure."
2nd Corinthians 12.21 NLT

Confession of sexual sin by itself, even honest confession, is not enough. Self-disclosure without repentance, as a form of accountability, indicates an unhealthy dependence on those to whom our confession is directed. Lasting change, not weekly penance, is the hallmark of real recovery.

The Myth of God-Dependency

We commonly use our perception (or should I say misperception?) of God for our own purpose and to our personal advantage. The Bible says, "No one has ever seen God, not so much as a glimpse" (John 1.18 *The Message*), and yet we plaster God's face all over our private agenda by wrongly crediting Him for the plans of our own making, and later blaming Him and others (anyone but ourselves) when they do not work out. Like the two preceding "Myths," dependency on God is tricky because of the obvious truth contained in this (and every) myth. I must depend upon God, but not

31

to the exclusion of taking the action He requires of me. God-dependency becomes a false precept when used as an excuse for inaction in the face of clear and godly direction.

When Peter stood on the boat's edge in the dark morning hours on a choppy Galilean sea, Jesus issued a command to "Come!" Matthew records, "And climbing out of the boat, Peter started walking on the water and came toward Jesus" (Matthew 14.29 HCSB). God did not push Peter out of the vessel, nor did Jesus grab the disciple's hand and pull him into the turbulent deep. It was Peter's call to faith and action, and his alone. No one, not even Jesus, could take that step of obedience for him.

When I was in college at the University of Washington, I took a class in Geology. I did not care for the subject matter, and so chose not to study. As a new Christian, I assumed God was going to take care of everything for me. I still cringe at the memory of what I am about to tell you. During the final exam, I prayed asking God to guide me to the correct answers. I guessed on every single test question. To add to my pitiful academic laziness, I decided to "witness" to the professor and wrote notes in the test margins: "God bless you, teacher" and "Jesus loves you" and "God is good." Why I thought that type of messaging would be helpful, on any level, is still a mystery to me. I hate to think of what must have gone through my college professor's mind as he placed the large red "F" on my final exam. My religious stupidity must have made for a good laugh at the faculty cocktail party.

Whatever happened to simple obedience? I am not playing a chess game with the Almighty. There is no need for me to create a strategy, analyze my moves, or anticipate His. I am not equal to God. Why should I consult myself or consider my preferences before taking the action He requires of me? According to the Bible, "...whoever knows the right thing to do and fails to do it, for him it is sin" (James 4.17 ESV). Christ's query resonates in my soul as both a fair question and one that inspires fear: "Why do you call me, 'Lord, Lord,' and do not do what I say?" (Luke 6.46 NIV).

As it pertains to sexual sobriety, could God's will for a man be any clearer?

"For this is the will of God, your sanctification: that you abstain from fornication [πορνεία]; that each one of you know

how to control your own body in holiness and honor, not with lustful passion..." 1st Thessalonians 4.3-5a NRSV

"For this is the will of God... that you abstain from πορνεία." I do not need to *think* about it, I just need to *do* it. "Abstain from πορνεία." How much easier it is to hold to my pseudo God-dependency, making Him responsible for my obedience, or blaming him for my disobedience.

Consider, for example, Paul's infamous "thorn in the flesh."

"Therefore, so that I would not exalt myself, a thorn in the flesh was given to me, a messenger of Satan to torment me so I would not exalt myself. Concerning this, I pleaded with the Lord three times to take it away from me. But He said to me, 'My grace is sufficient for you, for power is perfected in weakness.'" 2nd Corinthians 12.7b-9a HCSB

I've heard men explain that πορνεία was their "thorn in the flesh." These men justified their sin by attributing it to God. "I pleaded with the Lord three times to remove my overactive libido, but I still want my sex drug. Obviously, God has not taken this 'thorn' from me, so pornography must be my 'cross to bear.' I wish I didn't have sexual addiction in my life, but Jesus allows it to remind me that His 'grace is sufficient' and His 'power is perfected in my weakness' for women. Giving in to sexual temptation is God's way of keeping me humble by reminding me I am still not perfect. Therefore, I guess I will accept this defect as a part of His plan for me." Does this interpretation of Scripture sound suspect? Well, it should because it is; and I should know, because I've used it myself.

It has been said, "Without God, I can't. Without me, He won't." I have a responsibility which I cannot shirk. It is mine, and mine alone. Jesus cannot obey God for me. Obedience to the will of God is the role I am called to play in the story of my own recovery.

Addiction is a Theological Problem

The addict lives in a fantasy land filled with lies and heresies. Common half-truths he uses early in his addictive process include:

"I can fix myself."

"I'm not that bad. I just have to try a little harder."

"I can stop anytime I want to."

"I just need someone to talk to."

"I have accountability."

"This thing does not control me."

"I am not an addict."

"God will take care of it."

He wants to believe he can heal himself and stop acting out sexually, but he cannot. He may have periods of cleanness when he doesn't even think about sex, an objective fact that serves to further fuel his denial. But the temptation and sin always return. The man will again succumb to the lure of sex. The pattern is established. His good intentions and hard efforts amount to nothing.

Every step of self-healing embarked upon by the man stuck in the addictive cycle contains elements of truth. That's why it's so easy for the addict to deceive himself. All heretical belief systems contain truth particles. It's this combination of truth plus untruth that enables a user to embrace the believable parts of his heretical views while ignoring the convicting parts. He convinces himself that the portions he chooses to disregard, like the impact of his sexual exploits on his conscience, family, energy, time, and money, have no serious consequences. All addicts lie, first to themselves, then to others.

By definition, heresy is partial truth, or truth mixed with lies. If heretical teaching were pure falsehood, then no one, including the addict, would believe it. Mixing a little sugar with cyanide will make it taste better, but it will still kill you. The addict drinks the Kool-Aid® of his own propaganda every single day.

Trying harder, getting accountability, and relying on God are all valid biblical themes, but they can be so easily misapplied:

Personal effort *without trust in Jesus*
Accountability to others *without real repentance*
Reliance on God *without obedience to His commands*

Each one of these heretical thought patterns leads inevitably and most assuredly to death and destruction.

Orthodoxy is contrasted with heresy insofar as it maintains an element of mystery. The right path is not always clear, and is generally the harder path to take. An orthodox view of life requires us to depend on Jesus and walk in obedience without the benefit of readily available answers. There are no easy, obvious, or quick fixes. God's ways transcend our analysis and thought process. We cannot see the future nor predict the outcome of our actions.

"For as the heavens are higher than the earth, so are my ways than your ways and my thoughts than your thoughts." Isaiah 55:9 ESV

God will not allow us to figure Him out. He baffles, perplexes, disappoints, and even outrages us. When we think we 'get it,' we don't.

"The wind blows wherever it pleases. You hear its sound, but you cannot tell where it comes from or where it is going. So it is with everyone born of the Spirit." John 3.8 NIV

The Spirit of God is like the wind and, as Solomon explained, "…no one has power over the wind to contain it" (Ecclesiastes 8.8a NIV 2011). You cannot capture the wind in a box, even a theologically airtight one. God cannot be grasped because He is full of surprises. Some of His most astonishing bombshells become shockingly evident as we walk in faith, including:

The unfathomable depth of God's love for the addict.

The unlimited lengths to which God will go to redeem the undeserving.

The miraculous story every fallen soul may offer others in similar situations.

Like the woman caught in adultery, Jesus delivers simple hope for a life of healthy sexuality.

"I do not condemn you…. Go. From now on sin no more."
John 8.11 NASU

Perhaps the only real solution is trust in a loving, unpredictable, and surprising God who delivers hope instead of wrath. If this premise is true, then our theology must transition from the theoretical and academic to the personal and relational. In this new realm, I (thankfully) no longer get what I deserve and I slowly, very slowly, start to comprehend that my Father in heaven actually loves "a wretch like me."[10]

The beauty of a relationship with the Son of God is that He initiates it. All that is left for me to do is say "Yes" to His gracious offer of friendship. It's a gift and there's nothing I can do to earn or deserve it.

> *"For by grace you have been saved through faith; and that not of yourselves, it is the gift of God; not as a result of works, so that no one may boast."* Ephesians 2.8-9 NASU

When the apostle Paul first preached in the Roman colony of Philippi, a woman named Lydia believed his message and became an ardent follower of Jesus. Luke records, "The Lord opened her heart to respond to Paul's message" (Acts 16.14b NIV). Lydia did nothing to secure her eternal destiny. Rather, her salvation was the unexpected act of a gracious God who chose to "open her heart to respond" in faith.

Could it really be that easy? Can I actually get off the merry-go-round of lies and "sin no more"? Is it God's intention to "open [my] heart to respond" to Jesus and His plan of redemption for my troubled soul? Could addiction recovery be more about simple trust than my resolve, will power, determination, and performance?

---

[10] "Amazing Grace," 2nd line in hymn by John Newton, 1779.

4 ADDICTION TAKES YOU SOMEWHERE YOU DON'T WANT TO GO

Sexual addiction is a progressive sin. It will get worse. One bad sexual decision leads to another, worse decision – not at first, but eventually. Some guys assume they can plateau with πορνεία at a certain point of acceptableness. They hope to find and maintain that level of sin which is high enough to routinely get a small 'hit' from their sex drug, but low enough to avoid detection, or at least major disapproval, by God and their own conscience. They actually think that, in so doing, they can effectively manage their sin. They cannot. They have to kill it. Strong, decisive action must be taken to eliminate the addiction. You cannot argue, debate, or negotiate with a terrorist. Satan is a terrorist with one, and only one, aim… your complete annihilation. His objective is destruction and his strategy is addiction. Kill or be killed. Kill your addiction, or it will kill you.

Self-Validating Excuses

Some men excuse their sexual fantasies and carnal exploits as harmless and normal. The pursuit of πορνεία is accompanied by a myriad of creative rationalizations:

"I'm a man. It's what men do."
"God created me to want sex."
"I'm not hurting anyone."

"It's OK to look, as long as I don't touch."
"I can't stop. I've tried. It's not possible."
"I can stop anytime I want to."
"I am an extremely sexual being."
"The woman's body is a beautiful thing to be admired."
"My wife doesn't seem to mind."
"I can't imagine life without sex."
"I don't have a girlfriend or wife. What am I supposed to do?"
"I can control it. It's not getting any worse."
"It helps me be a better lover to my wife."
"Everyone else is doing it."
"Our culture throws it in my face. What can I do?"
"It's summertime and it's hot. The girls are wearing less."
"I have an overactive libido."
"Spandex! What can I say?"
"Don't those women know what they do to me?"
"It's fine to watch the birds fly by, as long as I don't let them build a nest in my hair."
"The devil made me do it!"[11]

As foolish as some of these statements sound, every one of these excuses contains an element of truth, making it easy for the addict to lie to himself. He is avoiding the real truth which is simply this... *he must have illegitimate sexual experiences*. The more dangerous, risky, exotic, explicit, and forbidden, the better. Nothing else offers the exhilaration, intoxication, and release he craves. The lure of the thrill is too much for him. It's an irresistible rush of dopamine promising (and delivering) immediate and indescribable pleasure. It's coming at him with the unrelenting sexual force of a Category 5 hurricane. He cannot stop his pursuit of πορνεία. He wants it and will have it at any cost.

What the addict doesn't know, or refuses to believe, is that sex addiction is progressive. It will spiral out of control and plummet depths of horribleness that would sicken the sex-drug user if he could view his future. He is on a path that eventually leads to a dirty,

---

[11] From comedian Flip Wilson's (1933-1998) character Geraldine Jones' famous lines: "The devil made me buy this dress," "When you're hot, you're hot; when you're not, you're not," and "What you see is what you get."

dark destination, terminating at violent sex, orgy sex, public sex, animal sex, child sex, or in extreme cases, death sex by such means as necrophilia, electrostimulation, and erotic asphyxiation. On the threshold of unspeakable acts such as these, the mere mention of which should cause anyone's stomach to churn, it's too late for the addict. He's now near the end of his joy ride and faces public humiliation, loss of family and income, incarceration, and death.

"Do not be deceived: God cannot be mocked. A man reaps what he sows. Whoever sows to please their flesh, from the flesh will reap destruction..." Galatians 6.7-8a NIV 2011

I shall never forget meeting a young man whose sin escalated to the place where he sexually fondled his own little girls. He was on his way to prison, and he knew it was the right place for him to be. He wondered if he would ever see his precious children again. Please do not say, "I would never do anything *that* bad." Every man who ever did "anything that bad" once believed he never would.

The problem of men becoming insanely stupid when preoccupied with bad sex is not new. It was the subject of 3,000 year old warnings like the one below:

"Before you know it, he's trotting behind her,
   like a calf led to the butcher shop,
Like a stag lured into ambush
   and then shot with an arrow,
Like a bird flying into a net
   not knowing that its flying life is over.
"So, friends, listen to me,
   take these words of mine most seriously.
Don't fool around with a woman like that;
   don't even stroll through her neighborhood.
Countless victims come under her spell;
   she's the death of many a poor man.
She runs a halfway house to hell,
   fits you out with a shroud and a coffin."
Proverbs 7.22-27 *The Message*

Self-validation in the face of sin is a form of deception, leading the addict further down a path of devastation and ruin. Every man's behavior points him in a specific direction. His direction determines his destination and his destination eventually becomes his destiny.[12] A man's destiny defines him to the world and leaves a posterity he can never change.

The man of God is determined to leave the world a better place than he found it. He is concerned about his influence on those who will follow in his footsteps. He considers the future and works backwards from there. He reverse engineers his life plan by making wise decisions today which he knows will define the future he envisions.

- Question: What *should* be inscribed on a man's tombstone?

- Answer: That which is memorialized in the hearts of those he left behind.

What will those words be…? "He Chased Women" or "He Chose God"? The good man imagines his destiny and makes choices today in keeping with his grand and final goal.

One of Israel's worst leaders, King Jehoram, "passed away to no one's regret" (2nd Chronicles 21.20 NIV), a sad but predictable fate for the person who lives without regard for the next generation. Nearly one thousand people attended my wife's funeral. Adonica "passed away to… [the] regret" of many because she showed great love and concern for those she was leaving behind, even before she knew she was dying of cancer. We all die, and what we do with our short, allotted time matters. It matters greatly. The wisest of all men, King Solomon, once said, "The end of a matter is better than its beginning" (Ecclesiastes 7.8 NASB) or, as my friend Greg Wright, says, "Live your epitaph, not your résumé." A wise man fully comprehends the fact that everything about his decisions this day will impact his future and the futures of those he loves, so he wisely chooses to act accordingly now.

Bad sex never satisfies. The pursuit of πορνεία has no endpoint beyond death. The addict cannot snatch the carrot swinging on the

---

[12] *Seven Pillars of Freedom*, by Dr. Ted Roberts, Pure Desire Ministries, © 2009, p. 41.

stick just inches beyond his grasp but, against all reason, he keeps on trying. He imagines there must be something more, a sexual nirvana, the ultimate fantasy, the climax to beat all climaxes. He will find it or die trying, and die he will for "there is a way that seems right to a man, but its end is the way to death" (Proverbs 14.12 ESV). This is the 'novelty effect' in action. Internet porn overstimulates the brain by providing an unending supply of sexual novelty. Perhaps it is not sex alone that drives an addict, but rather the search for new and exciting forms of sex he has not yet imagined. Unopposed and given enough time, this addictive quest can prove deadly... death to careers, death to relationships, death to integrity, death to hope, death to dreams and their future fulfillment, and even death to the gifts of temporal and eternal life.

I know a man who sat in front of his computer screen trying to locate the perfect sexual image all night long. Time passed without his notice, until it was 6:00 a.m. and he had to get ready for a day's work with no sleep. I know a family doctor who lost a successful fifteen year practice because he could not stop viewing pornography at his medical office. I know a woman who considered suicide when she discovered her husband was viewing pornography. I know a man whose wife threatened divorce if he did not stop his porn habit. He didn't stop. He just got more secretive. She found out and divorced him, just like she said. I know a young man who actively masturbated to online porn for years, but could not get an erection on his wedding night. I know a grown man who wept uncontrollably when sharing his story of being sexually abused by an older relative when he was a pre-teen. I know a man who crashed his car because he was staring at a woman on the street rather than watching the road. I know a man who stripped at a nude beach while conducting his favorite pastime of voyeurism. When he returned to the parking lot, his car was stolen. (That last guy was me.)

Make no mistake, πορνεία steals life, energy, hope, and happiness, just as the Bible foretells: "For the wages of sin is death..." (Romans 6.23a NIV).

Sensitization and Tolerance

The deeper a man slips into πορνεία's whirlpool, the stronger

41

the pull of his cravings becomes. This brain process is called *sensitization.* The user gradually becomes more sensitive to sensual stimuli, so it takes less to arouse his sexual appetite. He peers into the sky and sees only clouds in the shape of a woman's breasts. Everywhere he looks he sees and is enticed by sex. As his brain becomes sensitized to the lure of bad sex, he sees opportunity everywhere and will be tempted to take inappropriate, hazardous, and possibly even illegal, actions. The line between reality and fantasy becomes seriously blurred and the addict unknowingly begins to fall apart internally. He may interpret a female's attire or manner as an invitation for a sexual rendezvous, just like it occurs in his delusional dreams. At some crucial point, the man overcome by lust will cross previously self-forbidden boundaries of gender, age, law, and ethics. Job loss, broken marriages, rejection by his children, irreparable damage to his reputation, registered sex offender status, and jail time may all be in his future.

The addict who does not get help will spiral out of control. As his *sensitization* to sexual activity increases, so does his *tolerance.* While it takes less to stimulate the user's sexual hunger, it takes more to satisfy it. The addict cannot plateau at an acceptable level of dabbling in forbidden sex for one simple reason: *wrong sexual pleasure never satisfies.* He must look for and find something better. Yesterday's five minutes of soft porn is today's hour of hardcore, and, while tomorrow's outcome remains a mysterious unknown, his addictive behavior is guaranteed to escalate. "Over time, with enough consistent flooding of our brains with this dopamine, our dopamine receptors actually numb themselves as a defense mechanism against overloading... we need more extreme porn to get off."[13] The journey is incremental and almost imperceptible. The man in pursuit of πορνεία "is getting excited more and more easily but experiencing less and less fulfillment. Welcome to total insanity!"[14]

Sexual temptation has existed for a very long time, perhaps since the beginning of the world, but this generation is unique. With the development of the Internet, we now have graphic pornography

---

[13] *"Porn-induced erectile dysfunction (yes, it's a real thing)"*, video by Noah B. E. Church, author of <u>WACK: Addicted to Internet Porn</u>, 2014.
[14] Ibid, *Seven Pillars of Freedom*, p. 34.

at our fingertips. Most high schoolers have smart phones.[15] What do you think curious boys use their phones for? Do you imagine a typical14-year-old male has the capacity to say "no" to the sexual bait dangling within easy reach? Moms and dads may want to consider implementation of two simple rules for the ultimate benefit of teenagers who cannot possibly grasp the power of sex for at least another decade:

1. Don't give smart phones to dumb kids.
2. When it comes to sex, all kids are dumb.

Parents have a responsibility to defend youngsters in the home from πορνεία's blatant assault on their developing brains. Instead of protecting our children (e.g., by offering them 'old school' flip phones, dumbing down their smart phones, adding porn filters, limiting Internet access, etc.), we have adopted culture's value system because it's easier than standing up to a screaming teen's mantra, "All the kids at school have smart phones. Why can't I?" We have chosen to remain naïve and permissive and, in so doing, created a generation of young men and women addicted to erotica. Pornography is more readily available than at any other time in the history of the world, but the light is glimmering on the horizon.

Cultural Shift in Society

In a recent TIME magazine article, Belinda Luscombe made this observation:

"A growing number of young men are convinced that their sexual responses have been sabotaged because their brains were virtually marinated in porn when they were adolescents. Their generation has consumed explicit content in quantities and varieties never before possible, on devices designed to deliver

---

[15] "51 percent of high school students carry a smartphone with them to school every day, compared to 28 percent of middle school students." From *"Living and Learning with Mobile Devices – What Parents Think About Mobile Devices for Early Childhood and K-12 Learning,"* Grunwald Associates LLC, Learning First Alliance with support from AT&T, 2013.

content swiftly and privately, all at an age when their brains were more plastic – more prone to permanent change – than later in life. These young men feel like unwitting guinea pigs in a largely unmonitored decade-long experiment in sexual conditioning. The results of the experiment, they claim, are literally a downer."[16]

The writer is referring to what some are calling porn-induced erectile dysfunction (PIED). When confronted with an opportunity to have actual sex with a real female partner when he was in high school, one interviewee stated, "There was a disconnect between what I wanted in my mind and how my body reacted." He could not "get the necessary hydraulics going"[17] and attributed this unpleasant phenomenon to PIED.

Gabe Deem, founder of Reboot Nation, explains, "I was told that porn would be sex positive, but it turned out to be completely sex negative because it gave me a limp noodle."[18] Deem is an advocate of sex education for young people who need to understand the negative effects of porn on a child's mind. "Education is the key... I stayed away from hard drugs as a teenager because I knew of the negative effects."[19] According to Deem, an awareness campaign designed to educate teenagers can work to help curb the new drug of pornography.

Others agree. On Tuesday, March 19th, 2016, the state of Utah officially declared online porn as a new health crisis. Governor Gary Herbert signed a resolution declaring pornography a public health hazard that harms both individuals and society. The nonbinding resolution calls for research, education, and policy changes to address "the pornography epidemic that is harming the citizens of Utah and the nation."[20]

---

[16] *"Porn and the Threat to Virility – The first generation of men who grew up with unlimited online porn sound the alarm,"* Belinda Luscombe, TIME magazine, Vol. 187, No. 13, April 11th, 2016, pp. 40-47.

[17] Ibid, p. 42.

[18] Netflix Original - Chelsea, *"Perils of Porn & Rachel Bloom's Big Year,"* 2016 Season 1, Episode 2.

[19] Ibid.

[20] *Concurrent Resolution on the Public Health Crisis*, 2016 General Session, State of Utah, Chief Sponsor: Todd Weiler, House Sponsor: Curtis Oda.

"Fight the New Drug" with its mission to "raise awareness on the harmful effects of pornography through creative mediums," targets youth with stellar graphics, science, facts, personal accounts, and compelling taglines like:

"Porn is to sex what bathroom graffiti is to art."
"Pixels will never love you back."
"If you look at what is fake for too long, you'll begin to find faults in what is real."
"Pro-sex, Anti-Porn"
"P.O.R.N. (Phony Objectifying Reductionist Nonsense)"
"Choose love, not porn."
"Sex is personal, not digital."
"We are what we watch."
"XXX lies."
"Porn fuels sex trafficking."
"People are not parts."
"When sex becomes easy to view, love becomes difficult to find."
"Love says, 'You're the only one for me.' Porn says, 'There's someone sexier out there.'"
"Real men don't have time to search for women online. They're too busy searching for ways to love the woman in front of them."
"Porn can't kiss you, hold you, cry with you, laugh with you, start a family with you, love you, grow old with you."
"Why is it that society unanimously condemns rape & abuse, yet openly consumes pornography that depicts both & worse?"[21]

John Mayer is a seven time Grammy award winning songwriter, music producer, and performer. His honest self-disclosure in an early 2010 interview with *Playboy* magazine epitomizes this generation's affinity with online porn. Soon after it was published, Mr. Mayer humbly and publicly apologized for his remarks in the interview as an attempt to be "witty" or "clever," stating his ambition to become a "possible future grownup." After

---

[21] Find ways to fight the new drug at http://www.fightthenewdrug.org.

reading some of John Mayer's comments below, try to cut this celebrity a little slack. He was a young man at the time of the interview, and dealing with fame of the sort you and I will likely never experience or be forced to endure. If you follow his music, you will detect his personal growth as an artist in the evolution of his craft (e.g., *"Shadow Days"* and *"Love is a Verb"* on his 2012 "Born and Raised" album). I am impressed with this man's honest journey.

"I'm a self-soother... By the way, pornography? It's a new synaptic pathway. You wake up in the morning, open a thumbnail page, and it leads to a Pandora's box of visuals. There have probably been days when I saw three hundred vaginas before I got out of bed.

"Internet pornography has absolutely changed my generation's expectations. How could you be constantly synthesizing an orgasm based on dozens of shots? You're looking for the one photo out of 100 you swear is going to be the one you finish to, and you still don't finish. Twenty seconds ago you thought that photo was the hottest thing you ever saw, but you throw it back and continue your shot hunt and continue to make yourself late for work. How does that not affect the psychology of having a relationship with somebody? It's got to.

"I grew up in my own head. As soon as I lose that control, once I have to deal with someone else's desires, I cut and run. I'm pretty culpable about being hard to live with. I have had a good run of imagining things into reality. I've got a huge streak of successes based on my own inventions.

"I can invent things really well. I mean, I have unbelievable orgasms alone. They're always the best. They always end the way I want them to end. And I have such an ability to make believe, I can almost project something onto my wall, watch it and get off to it: sexually, musically, it doesn't matter. When I meet somebody, I'm in a situation in which I can't run it because another person is involved. That means letting someone else talk, not waiting for them to remind you of something interesting you had in mind.

"...during sex, I'm just going to run a filmstrip. I'm still masturbating...Rather than meet somebody new, I would rather go home and replay the amazing experiences I've already had. "...I'm more comfortable in my imagination than I am in actual human discovery. The best days of my life are when I've dreamed about a sexual encounter with someone I've already been with. When that happens, I cannot lay off myself."

John Mayer's moral standards are not mine, but I respect the man. In the *Playboy* interview, he unapologetically told it exactly like it was for him in that moment, and probably for countless other men who would rather enjoy solo-sex than go to the trouble or risk the unhappiness of pursuing, creating, or fixing a real, live relationship with a real, live woman.

Besides the fact that Mr. Mayer is not a professing follower of Jesus, what's the main difference between this celebrity and many Christian men in unhappy, sexless marriages who secretly use porn? The answer is simple... John Mayer is honest. "According to the research approximately 64 percent, or two thirds, of U.S. men admit to viewing porn at least monthly, with the number of Christian men nearly equaling the national average."[22] The majority of Christian men are doing exactly the same thing as John Mayer, but keeping it a secret. They are lying to themselves and to their significant others. They have become two people in one... the outside man they wish to portray publicly, and the inside man they presume will be rejected if others meet him. Therefore, they must hide their inner man at all costs. Transparency and intimacy required for authentic relationships becomes a forgotten ideal. The irony is that millions of inner men would love to come out of hiding and meet each other; to embark on their journeys of self-discovery and together gain the confidence to quash πορνεία once and for all. Instead these men live independently, keeping intimate company only with the other side of themselves. Their dual personalities are systematically killing them and slowly destroying any hope for real relationships.

This incongruity between a man's belief system and his behavior patterns is a setup for mental instability. Fear of exposure drives him deeper into isolation and, of course, widens the gap between opposing inner forces. He perceives himself as a liar and a social

---

[22] *"Christian men view porn almost as much as non-Christians."* Joseph Pelletier, ChurchMilitant.com, January 18th, 2016.

outcast. He hopes for, but remains unassured of, God's love and forgiveness. He is overwhelmed with feelings of hypocrisy, a condition that hamstrings the man's efforts to effectively serve his family, church, and community.

The Christian, who is active in his sex addiction, may seek to resolve the inner conflict by forming separate personas as the occasion requires. He assumes his 'bad self' character when he wants to view pornography and masturbate, yet identifies as a 'good guy' with his brothers and sisters at church. If a man's contrasting value systems begin to function independently, he is in danger of becoming 'two-men-in-one.' The addict may choose not to recognize his duplicity by living in denial for a time but, in moments of clarity, he concludes that it is not possible to satisfy both his desire for πορνεία and his hunger for God. This realization pushes him to the emotional brink where the dark pit of despair and utter aloneness beckons him like a siren of final destruction. Could God's concern for our mental wellbeing be, in part, the reason Jesus warned, "No one can serve two masters" (Matthew 6.24 NAS)?

A man of God addicted to porn is trapped in an impossible situation. He cannot boldly proclaim Jesus who sets captives free when he cannot get himself untangled from the tentacles of πορνεία. How can he inspire his sons and daughters to be sexually clean when he keeps a hidden stash of favorite pornography on his laptop? In 423 Men we say, "You can't *get* clean until you *come* clean." Everything starts with the truth and, of course, Jesus promised, "The truth will set you free" (John 8.32b ESV).

The pursuit of πορνεία brings death. You will die in your never-ending hunt for hedonistic pleasure. God's plan brings vibrant, abundant, everlasting, and joy-filled life.

"For the wages of sin is death, but the gift of God is eternal life in Christ Jesus our Lord." Romans 6.23 NIV

Perhaps you agree, or want to believe, that nothing satisfies like the real thing, but you have fallen under the weight of sexual addiction and have concluded you can never wrench yourself free.

Please read on. There is hope.

5 YOU CAN RECOVER, BUT NOT ALONE

John Mark Comer is an outstanding preacher at Bridgetown Church in Portland, Oregon. He is known for humorous anecdotal quips like "'Jesus' is the correct answer to almost any question you hear in the church. If you can't think of anything else to say, say 'Jesus,' and you'll almost always be right." Jesus, of course, is the answer to the sin of the world. Among religious leaders and prophets, He stands alone as one claiming to be "the way and the truth and the life" (John 14.6 NIV). John's gospel opens with, "In the beginning was the Word, and the Word was with God, and the Word was God... And the Word became flesh, and dwelt among us..." (John 1.1, 14 NAS). According to the biblical witness, Jesus is God and has, therefore, earned the right to offer a solution to all that ails His earthly domain. Unfortunately, if the statistic noted in the last chapter is true, and the majority of Christian men are using porn, then something's amiss. The institution Christ established with the mandate, "...I will build my church, and the gates of Hades shall not prevail against it" (Matthew 16.18 NKJV), has not been successful in keeping πορνεία out of its ranks.

At first glance, it appears that either Jesus is not the answer to the question of πορνεία or the stats are incorrect. Based on my many years of experience working with men in the church, I do not disagree with the statistics. I am, of course, reluctant to take issue with the words of Jesus, so I am forced to another, perhaps more subtle, conclusion. Could it be that the problem is not with Jesus or

His power over sin, but with our theologically bent and faulty perception of Jesus?

<u>Who is Jesus?</u>

Many Christians behave as though they consider themselves to be the Lone Ranger with Jesus as their sidekick, Tonto. These believers have an agenda, and they expect Jesus to help them complete it. Jesus is an important tagalong, whose input is valid and helpful most of the time. In a pinch, "Tonto Jesus" is there to bail them out, but as a rule, Lone Ranger Christians can handle things themselves. They are the hero of their own story, not Jesus.

We have a saying in 423 Men. "You can overcome sexual sin, but you cannot do it alone." Many Christian addicts give verbal assent to this truism, but are quick to explain, as I've heard some say, "I have Jesus and that's enough. Me and Jesus can get the job done." Believers who struggle with sexual temptation often quote popular verses like, "I can do all things [like kick the porn habit] through Him who strengthens me" (Philippians 4.13 NAS). The misapplication of this Scripture text easily validates "The Myth of Self-Dependency" described in Chapter 2. For many self-starter personalities, Philippians 4.13 boils down to three words: "I can do," which is a prevalent theme in motivational self-talk but entirely misses the context of this biblical passage. Paul wrote or dictated these words during his detainment, probably in Rome, around AD 61. He was endeavoring to encourage the Philippian church by his example of having learned the secret of both hunger and abundance. Neither adversity nor prosperity would affect Paul's attitude, for he had "learned to be content in whatever circumstances" he found himself (4.11). "I can do all things" was not a mantra for success, nor was it written to help men stop looking at porn on the Internet. These words, rather, were a testament to the value of contentment in all circumstances.

Here's a more applicable verse for men enslaved to πορνεία:

"...we are no longer to be children, tossed here and there by waves, and carried about by every wind of doctrine, by the trickery of men, by craftiness in deceitful scheming; but speaking the truth in love, we are to grow up in all aspects into

*Him, who is the head, even Christ, from whom the whole body,
being fitted and held together by that which every joint supplies,
according to the proper working of each individual part, causes
the growth of the body for the building up of itself in love."*
Ephesians 4.14-16 NASB

Paul produced his letter to the Ephesian church, also likely from
his prison in Rome, to remind its members to be "diligent to preserve
the unity of the Spirit" (4.3) among the members of the church.
Unity is achieved, according to the apostle, when all believers in the
local church are operating in their own giftedness and growing in
their appreciation for and involvement in the body of Christ.

Jesus is not a cosmic bellhop or a useful sidekick. He is the head
of His body. Together believers form the body of Christ. Jesus is the
head, we are the body. If "the proper working of each individual
part, causes the growth of the body" (4.16) enabling us to "grow up
in all aspects into Him, who is the head, even Christ" (4.15), then it
follows that we cannot overcome our addictions alone. We need the
proper functioning of the body of Christ. Without interactive support
from members of His body, we will never get better or mature. I can
"grow up in all aspects into Him, who is the head, even Christ," but
I cannot do it without "the whole body" and "the proper working of
each individual part." That is a proper biblical way of saying, "I can
overcome sexual sin, but I cannot do it alone." I need the body of
Christ. Without my brothers in recovery, I will never achieve sexual
health.

'Me and Jesus' is not the answer. The real answer is 'Jesus, His
body, and I.' 'Me and Jesus' is religious code for 'me alone.' It is
the 'I-can-do' man's way of remaining isolated and detached from
authentic fellowship with brothers who can help. Jesus cannot be
separated from his body. Our Lord is not a floating head. He is
connected to His people. Christ in His "fullness" (Ephesians 1.23)
is comprised of both His head and His body, His Presence and His
community. We cannot have Jesus without "the communion of
saints."[23] No church... no Jesus. We will not overcome sexual
addiction if we remain secluded and determined to topple πορνεία
by ourselves and with our theologically inadequate understanding of

---

[23] Article 9 of *"The Apostle's Creed"* dating back to the 4th century AD.

Jesus. We need *all* of Jesus, including "His body, the fullness of Him who fills all in all" (Ephesians 1.23 NAS). We cannot find the healing we seek without loving, caring, believing people on the journey of recovery with us.

423 Men is a visible expression of the body of Christ for the addict. Men in recovery purify themselves *together* from the contaminating influence of sexual sin. Paul did not admonish each follower of Jesus to singularly 'purify himself.' Rather, the Apostle issued a collective command to "purify ourselves," implying that a community of faith was necessary to achieve the holiness God demands.

> *"...dear friends, let us purify ourselves from everything that contaminates body and spirit, perfecting holiness out of reverence for God."*
> 2nd Corinthians 7.1 NIV

We can overcome sexual sin, but we cannot do it alone.

Tell the Truth

In 423 Men we try to tell the truth. We don't sugarcoat, pose, pretend, defend or excuse ourselves, over-explain, understate, dismiss, minimize, rationalize, justify, deflect, misdirect, or mislead. We simply tell the truth about our sexually addictive behavior patterns. During meetings, members report on their previous week's successes and failures with sexual sin and lust issues. Overgeneralized statements about "acting out" are not acceptable, nor do we tolerate graphic detail which could sexually arouse listeners. Group members are simply required to confess and take responsibility for their sins in the presence of empathetic and supportive brothers. This transparent and honest process has an immediate freeing effect and has prompted some members to refer to their time in group as "real church." Imagine the spiritual power available to authentic and truthful Jesus followers who meet Him in a "real church" setting, such as a high functioning recovery group.[24]

---

[24] 423 Men does not replace the church. The program was birthed in a particular church, formerly called Solid Rock in Tigard, Oregon, and members are strongly

Who Can I Trust?

I must know and be known for significant relationships to occur. Sexual sin thrives in isolation and secrecy. I cannot heal without dependable and loyal friends in recovery who show up every week to hear my story and share their own. I must confess my sins, but not with everyone. I should be selective in my choice of confidants. Those with whom I bare my soul, share my life, and fully disclose my secrets must be trustworthy. 423 Men members prove they are worthy of trust by protecting each other's anonymity and confidentiality. *Anonymity* refers to the identity of group members. *Confidentiality* pertains to what members say in group.

Sometimes anonymity or confidentiality is broken accidentally, without malice or ill-intent. In the approximately sixteen years I have been involved in sexual recovery ministry, I have never seen or heard of a guy who intentionally violated the anonymity or confidentiality of another member. I have seen it happen accidentally on rare occasion, but never on purpose. The bonds of loyalty, friendship, love, and trust built between brothers in recovery are way too strong to make an infraction of this kind a common occurrence. A man who breaks confidentiality by revealing personal information with people outside of group could, depending on the circumstances, be asked to leave 423 Men.[25]

Addicts are best served by other addicts, especially when trust is established. Brothers in recovery are uniquely equipped to help other brothers in recovery. A man who is actively engaged in wrong sexual behavior may find little help from counselors, well-meaning Christians, pastors, family members, or even close friends. These people may possess a trustworthy character, but without a shared experience of sexual addiction it is difficult for them to offer usable and worthwhile advice. They are simply not competent to do so.

---

encouraged to join to a local church. 423 Communities offers support to any church or organization wishing to establish a sexual recovery ministry.

[25] There are exceptions to the confidentiality rule. If a member communicates an intention to harm himself or others, reveals that he is sexually involved with a minor, or the abuse of an elderly person or person with handicaps, this information would lead to the breaking of confidentiality with appropriate authorities (e.g., police, family and victim services, suicide units, etc.) as described in the *"423 Agreement"* included in the Appendix of this book.

In the world of business, trustworthiness is established with the "Two C's." Professionals build trust by virtue of both their character and competence. You would not choose a surgeon of great moral character cutting on you if he never attended medical school. Similarly, you would not select a highly competent financial advisor who was a thief. The men of 423 prove their *character* by loving and caring for each other, while maintaining strict confidentiality. They demonstrate their *competence* by the telling and hearing of shared experiences. This is how we provide effective pastoral care to one another in a 423 Men recovery group. We shepherd the sheep of our recovery flock by use of the "Two C's," taking our inspiration from King David's example as the leader of a great nation a thousand years before the birth of Christ:

> *"And David shepherded them with integrity of heart* [character]*; with skillful hands* [competence] *he led them."* Psalm 78.72 NIV

A man struggling with sexual addiction needs brothers in recovery from whom he can gather strength and for whom he can be strong. True recovery is a 'give and take' enterprise. The addict must receive *and* offer help if he is to create trust and find healing.

One of the best ways to develop trust among the members of a recovery community is to listen more than we talk. "No one is allowed to cross-talk, offer advice, or preach at other members of the group. This is a subtle way of introducing shame and judgment. 423 Men offers a safe and grace-filled environment for men to confess their sexual sin with other men in recovery who offer empathy, compassion, mercy, and strength."[26] Some new members have inquired, "If we can't give or receive advice and wise counsel in group, then what's the point of meeting together?" The point is this: there is great release of spiritual power in the hearing and telling of true stories. Full disclosure in the context of people committed to the success of each member of their recovery group yields astonishing results:

---

[26] Items 12 and 13 on *"Typical 423 Meeting"* included at the Appendix of this book.

When I hear a man honestly confess his sins, I am endeared to that man.
When I hear about his failures, I learn from his example how not to be.

When I hear about his successes, I am encouraged to become successful in my fight for purity.

When I share my history of sexual sin with non-judgmental brothers, I feel safe.

When I am loved by men who accept me in spite of my sin, I learn to trust others.

When I can trust frail men who love Jesus, I can more easily trust Jesus who holds the ultimate power over sin.

When I trust Jesus, I am renewed in my confidence to gain victory over my sin.

Trust your brothers in recovery. They will help you trust Jesus, according to whom, anything is possible when that trust is established.

> *"Yeshua said to him, 'What do you mean, "if you can"? Everything is possible to someone who has trust!'"* Mark 9.23 CJB

423 Men is a Christ-centered organization which integrates the best of commonly used recovery tools with the Bible and prayer. There are a variety of effective recovery formats for addicts. Help is available through non-church related, organizations like Alcoholics Anonymous (AA) and Sexaholics Anonymous (SA) which promote dependence upon "God" and a "Higher Power" or a personal "Power greater than ourselves."[27] All addicts need a recovery community. Some need intensive counseling or therapy in addition to weekly

---

[27] From step 2 of *"The Twelve Steps of Sexaholics Anonymous."*

group time. 423 Men is distinguished from other twelve-step programs by its commitment to the belief that Jesus Christ and His Church comprise the ultimate answer to every addiction. The remainder of this chapter will be devoted to the role of the church in the recovery process and the reason recovery doesn't always work, even in the Church of Jesus Christ.

Cultural Shift in the Church

I am privileged to have served as a volunteer providing administrative oversight and pastoral care to the men in sexual recovery programs at two large churches in Portland, Oregon. In both cases, about two or three years after launching the program, I witnessed a noteworthy shift in thought about sexual recovery in general, and the program in particular, by both the men in the program and outside observers. Early months and years of this ministry in both congregations felt shaky, as though we were on trial or in a probationary period. I heard questions regarding the validity of such a ministry. Looking back, the skepticism which typified the opinions of many in the church seems to me completely understandable. Providing a ministry for men who need help overcoming sexually addictive behavior patterns is untraditional at best, and possibly even detrimental to the reputation of the church. I heard of one gentleman who stated, "Those guys meet to get their jollies by sharing detailed stories of sexual exploits." Others were afraid naïve members would learn about new avenues of sexual sin from more experienced members of the group. Men who wanted help were reluctant to join, mortified at the prospect of being labeled as "sex addicts." We worked hard in those early years to protect every member's right to privacy. Anonymity and confidentiality was, and remains to be, a high value in 423 Men. We operated under the radar, as a subculture in the larger church culture, appearing somewhat clandestine and mysterious to the general church population. It seemed as though some congregants spoke with darting eyes and in hushed tones about "that sex group."

As men got better, they tended to speak more openly, with less fear of reprisal, about their journey of self-discovery. 423 Men slowly gained legitimacy. In time, the local church adopted the concept of sexual recovery as a bona fide ministry. Men began to wear their dedication to the program as a badge of honor and wives found renewed respect for their husbands who attended 423 Men. There was a measurable and positive shift in public opinion. Our image somehow migrated from a group for weak men with a 'sex problem' to a group of men with integrity fighting "the good fight" of purity (1st Timothy 1.18; 6.12 NIV 1984). We moved, in our own minds and in the minds of onlookers, from the pathetic to the powerful, from cowards to warriors, from boys to men. It became more commonly believed that the men in 423 differed from many other men in our community by virtue of their courage and humility in the admission of brokenness. As more men of strong reputations joined 423 Men, naysaying faded and the program was embraced as a 'value added' service to the local body of Christ. It became widely presumed that almost any man could use some help in the arena of sex, if he but dared to ask. Even pastoral staff joined the program, found help, and promoted it from the pulpit.

Leaders emerged in 423 Men who openly rejoiced in their newly found sexual sobriety and became passionate to help other men. Their willingness to actively shepherd hurting men affirmed and gave voice to an expression of St. Paul, "I take pride in my ministry" (Romans 11.13 NIV 2011). We began to "take pride" in the ministry of 423 Men. The whole experience of sexual recovery in the local church felt almost 'early church-like' insofar as the blessing of God was palpable. We were experiencing a revival of purity, "praising God and having favor with all the people. And the Lord added to their number day by day those who were being saved" from the bondage of sexual addiction (Acts 2.47 ESV).

I reiterate that the process in both churches described above took years. If you are considering a ministry of sexual recovery in your church, do not expect immediate results or widespread backing. Be aware that this endeavor will not, and cannot, happen quickly. It takes time to overcome objections, demonstrate value, and establish credibility. Be patient and consistent. Show respect to all and submit to your church leaders. Keep the pastor, elders, and staff apprised of your progress. Most of all, wait for a call by Jesus Himself before you attempt to implement any program like 423 Men. Assurance of His calling will reinforce your resolve during times of controversy and waning support. If you know Jesus wants you to help men overcome their attachment to πορνεία, then jump in with total abandon. Get your hands dirty. Persevere. Love the guys God brings your way. Make a difference and leave these men and your church in better condition than you found them. Most of all, trust Jesus who issued you a call to serve in this specific way. He will open and close doors of opportunity before you.

"He who is holy, who is true, who has the key of David, who opens and no one will shut, and who shuts and no one opens, says this: 'I know your deeds. Behold, I have put before you an open door which no one can shut...'" Revelation 3.7-8a NAS

The 'Fizzle Factor'

There is an easy alternative to the highly structured methodology of 423 Men. Some guys may prefer to gather unofficially for "accountability." They recognize the lure of πορνεία and want help in the battle. They start small with a couple close friends, pick a time, and agree to meet regularly. This seems like a good idea at first, then life happens. The grassroots, organic approach to sexual recovery is met with limited success because of family scheduling conflicts, unmanaged expectations, and loss of interest, especially when the measurement of success is as intangible (and as easy to lie about) as sexual sobriety. There is a logistical price to pay for ongoing ministry, and few people have the stamina to finish what they start. I call this phenomenon the 'fizzle factor' which is high when it comes to small, informal accountability groups because the penalty for terminating groups like these is relatively inconsequential. In my experience, these groups come and go. Perhaps they accomplish their intended purpose, but they normally do not have staying power.

It takes a massive amount of work to organize and maintain a structured program like 423 Men. Critical elements of operation include:

Maintaining a fluid database for members
Monitoring weekly attendance
Conducting intake interviews

Creating member rosters
Facilitating transfer requests
Keeping an up-to-date waiting list
Making new member placements
Starting new groups as the need arises
Recruiting, developing, encouraging, and retiring leaders
Securing and cleaning facilities
Consulting with and keeping church leaders informed
Fielding inquiries and counseling members
Forming policies and implementing change
Staying educated

This ministry endeavor can be a fulltime job. It's no wonder those with an interest in sexual recovery ministry shy away from providing foundational leadership to a program-oriented effort like 423 Men. It's too much work. Why risk time, money, and energy to build a non-traditional, messy, controversial, and provocative ministry in sexual recovery? Why not, rather, quietly gather a couple friends, informally begin meeting, and see what happens? The only reason I can think of is the 'fizzle factor.' Organic efforts without strong structure, policy, and leadership in place often do not last and their impact, while possibly valid and effective, is short-lived.

The Revolutionary War patriot Thomas Paine commented, "Those who expect to reap the blessings of freedom, must, like men, undergo the fatigue of supporting it."[28] Nothing's free, especially not freedom from πορνεία. There's a price to pay for recovery from sexual addiction, just as there is a price to start and operate an effective program for men with sexually addictive behavior patterns. The benefits, however, are unmistakable and worth the effort. Just because a man wavers today in his steadfastness to achieve sexual sobriety now does not mean he will do so tomorrow, next week, or next year. When he is ready, 423 Men will still be there, Lord willing, to assist him on his journey to sexual freedom. We've had many men join 423 Men, quit, and later join again. That fact alone; that is, the consistent availability of recovery groups for the benefit of those who need help when they need it, is enough reason to pay

---

[28] Opening line in Chapter IV – "Philadelphia, Sept. 12, 1777" of Thomas Paine's *The American Crisis.*

the price for a well-structured and highly organized ministry of excellence led by recovering addicts who are devoted followers of Jesus.

The *Real* Reason Treatment Fails

It is not easy to overcome obstacles of lethargy, fear, and pride, grab your own scruff-of-the-neck, and force yourself to take the first step toward sexual healing. Locating a recovery group for men with sexually addictive behavior patterns, or starting and maintaining such a group, is wrought with challenges and far too many excellent-sounding reasons not to do so. The quest for recovery is unpleasant and the pursuit of πορνεία is too attractive. Are you sick and tired of your addiction? Perhaps you are now ready to pay the price of discomfort to make a change for the better. Help is available, but heed the Apostle's warning:

"Now finish the work, so that your eager willingness to do it may be matched by your completion of it..." 2nd Corinthians 8.11 NIV

Match your "willingness" to perform the noble work of recovery with your "completion" of it. Such a plan to find and get help requires resolute intentionality, an undivided heart, and the willingness to suffer. But it can be done and you can do it.

If 423 Men and other similar recovery programs work well and offer hope, why wouldn't every addict reach out for help? Perhaps the answer lies not so much in the array of typical excuses (e.g., lack of time, need, or interest), but in the real fear of losing the one thing that consistently delivers the comfort an addict craves... the drug itself. His hatred of πορνεία is only surpassed by his love for it.

I've always admired what Eric Clapton, Jimi Hendrix, and Stevie Ray Vaughn could do with a Fender Stratocaster. They possessed a remarkable and rare gift. I've listened to a lot of Clapton music (Yardbirds, Bluesbreakers, Cream, Blind Faith, Derek and the Dominos) and anticipated an insider's look at the life of one of the world's greatest bluesmen when his book, *Clapton – The Autobiography*, hit the bookstores in 2007. I found out my musical hero was more than a virtuoso. He was an addict. Clapton seriously abused sex, heroin, and alcohol and it nearly ruined his life. In 1982, at the age of thirty-eight, Eric finally admitted he had a problem and became willing to enter an alcohol treatment center.

> "On the flight over I drank the plane dry, so terrified was I that I might never be able to drink again. This is the most common fear of alcoholics. In the lowest moments of my life, the only reason I didn't commit suicide was that I knew I wouldn't be able to drink anymore if I was dead. It was the only thing I thought was worth living for, and the idea that people were about to try and remove me from alcohol was so terrible that I drank and drank and drank, and they had to practically carry me into the clinic."[29]

In a moment of clarity and truth, ask a porn addict how he might feel if, for the remainder of his life, he could never see or visualize another naked woman, other than his wife (if he is lucky enough to have one). I think you know the answer. The loss of his beloved πορνεία is a fate worse than the most horrible of deaths. The user cannot comprehend, nor will he try to imagine, life without his killer-of-pain. The unspeakableness of this thought horrifies him.

My good friend Dr. Lonnie Smucker has a saying about those who are not ready for sexual recovery. "Perhaps they need to leave group and go do a little more research." Lonnie is a medical doctor who has been working his own sexual recovery plan for years. He is an active leader in 423 Men and has helped many men and their families. Lonnie and I are of the same opinion that until the horrors of sexual addiction outweigh a man's love for it, he is not prepared for the rigors of recovery. He must be ready to say "goodbye" to that which he loves the most, his cherished πορνεία.

Letting go of your sex drug will be accompanied by a profound sense of loss and grief. You cannot bear this suffering by yourself; you need a recovery community. Isolation will kill you emotionally, and drive you back again and again to the destructive comfort and false hope bad sex offers.

You can overcome sexual sin, but you cannot do it alone.

---

[29] *Clapton – The Autobiography*, Eric Clapton, Broadway Books, 2007, p. 198.

6 INTERRUPTING THE PATTERN OF RELAPSE

The recovering addict must learn to properly distinguish between a temporary lapse of judgment and a consistent pattern of relapse. When I hear a man explain, "I'm doing great. I haven't looked at porn for three months," I usually inquire about his sexual history. I may learn that he isn't doing great at all. He was clean from pornography for three months prior to his last fall, and three months prior to that, and so on. In other words, he is on a quarterly relapse plan. He is surprised when I suggest that he expects, and even plans, to use pornography about every three months. That is his relapse pattern. There is no essential difference between this guy and the one who uses P&M (porn and masturbation)[30] every day. Both men are out of control sexually and engaged in a consistent pattern of relapse, albeit on different schedules. The initial goal for each man is to recognize, and then interrupt, his particular pattern of relapse. For the first guy, that's six months without using his sex drug. The other man's ambition early in recovery may be to last one week before falling. If they succeed, both have interrupted their individual relapse patterns and can build on their successes. With help from his brothers in recovery, each one will find hope to go further and last longer.

A singular lapse in judgment does not necessarily mean the addict has fallen back into his old pattern of relapse. However, if lapses occur routinely, they may indicate a new relapse pattern. The

---

[30] Also called PMO (pornography, masturbation, orgasm).

prophet Jeremiah inquired, "The heart is deceitful above all things, and desperately sick; who can understand it?" (Jeremiah 17.9 ESV). Apparently we do not, and may never, fully know ourselves, our motivations, or all the reasons for our behavior. Therefore, it's easy to self-deceive. The Lord knows me better than I know myself, a point which He clarifies in His divine response to Jeremiah's rhetorical question:

> *"I the LORD search the heart and test the mind, to give every man according to his ways, according to the fruit of his deeds."* Jeremiah 17.10 ESV

Even the most prolific New Testament writer, the Apostle Paul, expressed trouble understanding his own heart:

> *"We know that the law is spiritual; but I am unspiritual, sold as a slave to sin. I do not understand what I do. For what I want to do I do not do, but what I hate I do. And if I do what I do not want to do, I agree that the law is good. As it is, it is no longer I myself who do it, but it is sin living in me. I know that nothing good lives in me, that is, in my sinful nature. For I have the desire to do what is good, but I cannot carry it out. For what I do is not the good I want to do; no, the evil I do not want to do — this I keep on doing. Now if I do what I do not want to do, it is no longer I who do it, but it is sin living in me that does it.*

> *"So I find this law at work: When I want to do good, evil is right there with me. For in my inner being I delight in God's law; but I see another law at work in the members of my body, waging war against the law of my mind and making me a prisoner of the law of sin at work within my members. What a wretched man I am! Who will rescue me from this body of death? Thanks be to God — through Jesus Christ our Lord!*

> *"So then, I myself in my mind am a slave to God's law, but in the sinful nature a slave to the law of sin."* Romans 7.14-25 NIV 1984

If St. Paul attributed the mystery of his behavior to a "sinful nature," then so may we. We give in to our addictions, act out sexually, and pursue πορνεία because we are all prone to sin.

> *"If we say that we have no sin, we deceive ourselves, and the truth is not in us. If we confess our sins, he is faithful and just to forgive us our sins, and to cleanse us from all unrighteousness. If we say that we have not sinned, we make him a liar, and his word is not in us."* 1st John 1.8-10 KJV

We cannot claim to know ourselves without accepting the reality of a sin nature that plagues our souls. If "all have sinned and fall short of the glory of God" and if "there is none who does good, no, not one" (Romans 3.23, 12b NKJV), then we cannot separate our addiction from the sinful "desires of the flesh," which is why Paul admonished the Galatian church to "walk by the Spirit":

> *"But I say, walk by the Spirit, and you will not gratify the desires of the flesh. For the desires of the flesh are against the Spirit, and the desires of the Spirit are against the flesh, for these are opposed to each other, to keep you from doing the things you want to do. But if you are led by the Spirit, you are not under the law."* Galatians 5.16-18 ESV

Paul follows up his mandate by presenting a list of fifteen sample sins, all of which exhibit an aspect of the "desires of the flesh," (e.g., "impurity and debauchery; idolatry and witchcraft; hatred, discord, jealousy, fits of rage, selfish ambition, dissensions, factions and envy; drunkenness, orgies, and the like.) The pursuit of πορνεία, translated "sexual immorality," tops the list:

> *"Now the works of the flesh are evident: sexual immorality [πορνεία]..."* Galatians 5.19 ESV

The question, "Why do I act out sexually?" may never be fully answered, but we can arrive at the destination of God's choice on our path of self-discovery, and that's far enough. We can achieve sexual sobriety, and will be most successful on our journey if we adopt a sound theology of addiction initiated by the premise that every person, and therefore every addict, is a sinner. Recovery starts, then, with our need for God's forgiveness which is freely offered through the atoning work of Jesus Christ.

A Sexual Sobriety Line

A man needs a standard by which to measure his progress. We call this standard a "sexual sobriety line." A man's sobriety line is determined privately in his closet of prayer. Its development is a personal matter between the recovering addict and Jesus. In 423 Men, we expect each member to listen to and learn to trust the voice of his conscience as it directs him to modify his behavior. While a sexual sobriety line is specific to each man, it normally changes with the passage of time and evolves as the member grows in his recovery. Sobriety lines should be in writing and may typically include statements like, "No pornography and masturbation to sexual images on my computer," or "Stop visiting strip clubs after I get off work," or "Wait until our wedding night to have sex with my fiancée." Additionally, a man's line may include elements from his relapse prevention plan, such as, "Read my Bible each day," "Be kind to my wife and kids," and "Invite a brother from my 423 Men group out for coffee each week."

The purpose of a sexual sobriety line is to help quantify a member's recovery achievements. It becomes an objective standard by which he can easily determine his points of stabilization and new levels of sexual sobriety. Is he remaining above or falling below his "line"? "Each man will be asked to establish and share his personal sexual sobriety line with the members of the group" and the group will help "hold each member accountable to remain above his own sexual sobriety line during meetings."[31] A simple, short, and clearly written sobriety standard will keep a man from easily lying to himself about his addictive process, especially as he shares his "line" and sexual activities of the past week with the guys in his 423 Men group.

It should be noted that our sexual sobriety line is not a measurement of spirituality. Strict adherence to a legal code, even a

---

[31] Items 8 and 9 on *"Typical 423 Meeting"* included in the Appendix of this book.

purity standard of our own design, will never earn God's favor. Like the Sabbath in the time of Jesus, 'the sobriety line is made for man and not man for the sobriety line' (see Mark 2.27-28) and 'the Son of Man (not you nor I) is Lord of the sobriety line' (see Luke 6.5). Our "line," then, is nothing more than a guide and, like the Mosaic Law, it is a tutor leading us to faith in Jesus who alone can give us the grace to overcome the spirit of πορνεία.

> *"Therefore the Law has become our tutor to lead us to Christ, so that we may be justified by faith. But now that faith has come, we are no longer under a tutor."* Galatians 3.24-25a NASU

A well-written sobriety standard, then, guides us toward the goal of purity until we no longer need it. In the case of a typical addict, that may take several years of hard recovery work and a lifetime of vigilance, but it is achievable.

When a guy struggling with sexual addiction takes his family to a crowded beach on a hot summer day, he may need to recite his sobriety line every few minutes under his breath, "I will not sexualize pretty young women in bathing suits." However, that same man has no need for a line against theft and does not commonly frequent a convenience store uttering, "I will not steal a candy bar." Why not? The precept, "Thou shalt not steal" (Exodus 20.15 KJV), became ingrained in his young heart in the first few years of life. He now strolls down the candy aisle without the slightest temptation to shoplift. However, two other commandments gave him trouble from the time of puberty forward: "Thou shalt not commit adultery" and "Thou shalt not covet thy neighbor's wife" (Exodus 20.14, 17 KJV).

I may need a sobriety standard to assist me in the arena of sexual temptation until the day I die. Until a crowded beach on a hot day holds as little temptation for me as a candy aisle in a grocery store, I will endeavor to maintain a well-rehearsed sexual sobriety line. My personal goal, however, is not to live above my sexual sobriety line every single day for the rest of my life. Rather, it is to know Jesus better; to thrust myself upon His everlasting mercy and to depend upon His grace to consistently walk in sexual freedom.

A Relapse Prevention Plan

When the addict is aware of his relapse pattern, and remains free from πορνεία beyond the repeating cycle point, he starts to stabilize. Stabilization is an early step in breaking his cycle of shame. It is crucial at this juncture to have a strong, clearly written relapse prevention plan in place. Occasionally, the man walking in freedom from sexual sin may stumble and experience a small, although dangerous, moral failure (e.g., a second look or 'double-take,' a fleeting sexual memory, a single momentary bout with porn, etc.). If he is active in recovery, he will become instantly aware of his setback and the reasons for it. He will recognize his vulnerability and the threat of repeated failures leading to a major fall (e.g., sexual encounter with another person, indulging in porn for days, breaking the law with a prostitute, uncontrolled fantasies, etc.). If he chooses not to take the first infraction seriously, his lapse will soon escalate, and he will easily slip back into a full-fledged pattern of relapse. If, on the other hand, the addict takes full responsibility for his first sobriety breach and quickly implements his relapse prevention plan, he has a fair chance of avoiding a more serious transgression.

A relapse prevention plan is not an act of contrition born in the dark moments following relapse. Rather, it is a proactive blueprint for deliberate sobriety. The plan is developed with an awareness of a man's historic patterns of addiction. The recovering addict recognizes the emotional triggers which traditionally have awakened his cravings for bad sex, and he executes his plan before the moment of sexual crisis; that is, prior the point of no return. A relapse prevention plan is a written list of strategies uniquely designed to help the addict find success in his progressive realization of sexual sobriety. The plan is subject to change and will evolve as he matures in the recovery process. It's a guide map offering hope to the man traveling on the path of purity. Equipped with a sturdy relapse prevention plan, the recovering addict feels assured of reaching the summit of self-discovery with Jesus and his brothers in recovery. With this assurance embedded in his soul, a man finds determination to continue the journey of sexual sobriety, one step and one day at a time.

An effective relapse prevention plan begins with a well written and often quoted sobriety line. If a man falls below his sobriety line, his prevention plan jumps to action and includes, at a minimum, honest confession to Jesus; his wife, if married (or fiancée if engaged); and the men in his recovery group. The man's wife (or fiancée) is not his accountability partner, but she deserves to know. Confession can be embarrassing and usually difficult for all parties to hear, but if done with sincerity and humility, and without minimizing the severity, the honest admission of failure can act as a deterrent to future violations. It is a man of God's job to protect his family from the entrance of the insidious and dangerous spirit of πορνεία into his marriage and home. Protection is not accomplished by hiding the truth of this sin from his wife, but by exposing his sin and by preventing its future access at the gateway of his own mind. Recovery renews the addict's mental state so he is ultimately equipped to slam the emotional door and "flee πορνεία" when it presents itself at the threshold of his thought life.

"Do not be conformed to this world, but be transformed by the renewal of your mind..." Romans 12.2 ESV

Your relapse prevention plan will contain a personalized list of new habits, disciplines, and endeavors designed to draw you away from situations which fuel your bad sex drive. Engaging in new activities may seem threatening, at first. They will force you outside your comfort zone, and that is exactly where you need to go. Taking the first step toward positive change is never easy, but often results in increased motivation for more of the same.

Below is a short sample list of endless possibilities. Instituting change will help to disrupt your pattern of relapse. Be creative. Have hope and have fun:

- Make friends with those who model healthy sexuality
- Participate in a new hobby or sport
- Develop better communication skills
- Expand your social network
- Start a daily Bible reading plan
- Develop a stronger sense of self-awareness
- Set apart time each day for prayer and meditation

- Compile and verbalize a list of positive affirmations
- Contribute your time and resources to a local church
- Capitalize on successes for increased confidence
- Write out and review your personal goals
- Get a new job or career
- Start hiking and connect with nature
- Find a competent therapist
- Keep a journal to record your feelings and insights
- Plan a date night with your wife, kids, or friends
- Involve family members in your relapse prevention plan
- Attend lectures and book readings on recovery
- Exercise! Move your body! Learn how to dance
- Identify and reduce stressors
- Use the "Faster Scale" with a friend in recovery[32]
- Eat breakfast weekly with a group of friends
- Achieve balance in work, exercise, and sleep
- Develop new healthy food habits
- Avoid energy depletion and introduce 'margin'
- Make a list of emergency contacts for accountability
- Volunteer at a homeless shelter

My personal relapse prevention plan includes, among other positive activities, the writing of this book and the oversight of the 423 Communities recovery program. When I help other men, I am also helping myself stay on the path of purity.

The man who faithfully employs the use of his relapse prevention plan may get knocked down, but if he is determined, he will get back up and continue the fight for healthy sexuality. His gutsy comeback demonstrates great progress and a triumph of monumental proportions.

"... for the righteous falls seven times and rises again..."
Proverbs 24:16 ESV

---

[32] "The Faster Scale" is a proven self-diagnostic tool developed by Michael Dyer in his groundbreaking work, *The Genesis Process for Change*, 4th ed., 2006. It follows the acronym FASTER (Forgetting Priorities, Anxiety, Speeding Up, Ticked-off, Exhausted, Relapse) as an effective relapse predictor when used with Dyer's weekly "Commitment for Change" worksheets.

Plausible Deniability

"Each man is expected to fully and honestly disclose the nature of his sexual sin."[33] Honesty is the expectation in 423 Men, and yet we know that addicts lie...

By minimizing their sin ("It's not that bad. Everyone does it.")

By refusing to believe their sin is really a sin ("I think God approves, so it's okay.")

By omitting key details of the story ("I can't remember anything else.")

By giving themselves reasons to lie ("I don't want to hurt her.")

By categorizing their sin as accidental ("I was not aware. It caught me off guard.")

By making 'un-keep-able' promises ("I won't do it again. That was definitely the last time.")

No man lies to others without first lying to himself. Self-lies are accomplished in one of two ways: 1) by either convincing oneself that a lie is true, or 2) by deciding it is permissible to tell a lie. Both are lies.

My son-in-law, Matt Booth, is an excellent attorney and one of approximately forty outstanding leaders in 423 Men at A Jesus Church network. He explains a self-lie in legal terms. "Plausible deniability" refers to the lack of evidence necessary to prove an allegation. A typical addict is an expert at this legal game which he plays in his own head. He becomes adept at plausibly denying to himself an allegation of sexual misconduct even though it is true. For example, if I pick up a travel magazine in the dentist's office, I may hope (at a level of conscious awareness I wish to ignore) to catch a glimpse of girls in bikinis on a boat in some exotic location while I nonchalantly flip pages. This practice is called "trolling."

---

[33] Ibid, item 11.

When I find what I was really looking for, my denial sounds plausible, even to me: "I was just waiting to have my teeth cleaned and casually perusing a magazine in the lobby. How could I possibly know what I would find there?"

When the addict 'innocently' scans a magazine, channel surfs with his TV remote, checks out the latest and most popular YouTube videos, or indiscriminately previews movies on Netflix, the question is not, "Did I know what I would see there?" to which his technically correct answer is "No." When the erotic image appears, as it always will if the addict continues his media exploration long enough, his "plausible deniability" argument kicks in: "I did not know what I would find there." The statement is true, but laughable. The real truth is the addict did not *want* to know what he would find there and purposely placed himself in a position where he might get an 'accidental hit' from his sex drug while telling himself, "It wasn't my fault I saw a naked woman!"

Actually, it was his fault because the addict did not want to get real with himself. He chose not to reach to. a deeper level of awareness and ask the more telling question: "*Should* I have known?" or "Could I reasonably have known what I was about to see there?" The obvious answer is "Yes," if a little investigative due diligence had been pre-applied to his media viewing habits. Telling the truth at this level requires a man to stay awake and remain attentive, anticipating sexual temptations before they present themselves. It's far too easy to click into 'zombie mode' and sleepwalk through daily life, allowing ourselves exposure to high levels of πορνεία we would otherwise consider to fall below our sexual sobriety standard. This is the 'power of drift' in action.

"Test yourselves to make sure you are solid in the faith. Don't drift along taking everything for granted. Give yourselves regular checkups. You need first hand evidence, not mere hearsay, that Jesus Christ is in you. Test it out. If you fail the test, do something about it." 2nd Corinthians 13.5 *The Message*

"Therefore, we must pay much closer attention to what we have heard, lest we drift away from it." Hebrews 2.1 ESV

Don't be a drifter, zombie, or sleepwalker. Stay awake. Be attentive. Remain vigilant. "Plausible deniability" allows a man to justify small doses of πορνεία without having to take responsibility for his misconduct. The recovering addict who lies to himself in this way will eventually come to admit the truth if he consistently listens to the stories of his brothers in recovery and the voice of his own conscience.

There is nothing on this planet more exhilarating to me than the joy of observing a person getting free from the bondage of addiction. Witnessing honest self-disclosure from the lips of an addict is a priceless gift he chooses to offer the members of his recovery group. When an addict tells the truth, you should listen. The shame and compounding pain of sexual sin has become too much for him to bear. Ultimately, a man in recovery will come to the end of himself, and when he does, you are the blessed beneficiary. He's had his fill of divorces, angry ex-wives, unhappy kids, car wrecks, job losses, broken friendships, meaningless flings, unfulfilled potential, and feelings of self-loathing. He is confronted by the "Man in the Mirror"[34] and you are exceedingly privileged to witness the miraculous birth of his honest self-disclosure. The addict has arrived at Robert Johnson's "Crossroads"[35] and must make one of two choices. He will continue doggedly down the path of addiction and destroy himself, or he will cast himself upon the mercy of Jesus and at the feet of his brothers in recovery. The choice is his, and his alone. God will not make a man do the right thing. When the addict chooses Jesus and his brothers, well, there are few words to describe the glorious event. Jesus put it this way…

"…there will be more rejoicing in heaven over one sinner who repents than over ninety-nine righteous persons who do not need to repent." Luke 15.7 NIV

---

[34] "Man in the Mirror" was a hit song peaking at number 1 when released in January 1988. It was written by Glen Ballard and Siedah Garrett and popularized by Michael Jackson.

[35] American blues artist Robert Johnson recorded Delta Blues style "Cross Road Blues" in 1936. Although the lyrics make no reference to the transaction, myth has it that Mr. Johnson sold his soul to the Devil at the crossroads of US 61 and US 49 in Clarksdale, Mississippi, in exchange for his popular musical talents.

When a man makes the connection between his addictive behavior patterns and his unresolved emotional issues, a light bulb goes on in his brain. Angels rejoice. It's a miracle, a revelation, a moment of truth, an epiphany, an 'aha' event imparting a lifetime of hope. Nothing now matters more than his recovery and healing. The man has embarked on the journey of self-discovery, and there's no turning back. He doesn't want to turn back. He's getting free from πορνεία's godless grip, at last!

A man walking in freedom from sexual sin...

Can look others in the eye with confidence
No longer fears being discovered
Quits lying
Becomes the same guy on the inside as he is on the outside
Is not ashamed of himself
Is no longer enslaved to sex
Smiles sincerely at himself and others
Hears the voice of God's affirmation, "Well done, good and faithful servant!"[36]
Is an active force in advancing the Kingdom of God on earth
Thinks kindly and fondly of himself and others
Finds hope and a purpose for living
Becomes bold as a lion

For most guys, the benefits of freedom from slavery, under the heavy-handed tyranny of πορνεία, provide enough motivation to remain on the journey of self-discovery. 423 Men does not solve the emotional problems of every man, nor does it solve a man's every emotional problem, but it does offer hope. If a man can find sobriety after decades of sexual addiction, he is filled with optimism for a better future. He is able to advance with confidence to the front lines of ministry. He can make a difference and confidently leave the world a better place than he found it. He is fulfilling the Great Commission of Jesus to "go and make disciples of all nations" (Matthew 28.19 NIV). He now knows his life matters to the Lord and to others. He no longer feels like a pathetic addict or loser. He

---

[36] From Jesus' parable of the talents, Matthew 25.14-30 NIV (v. 23) and parallel passage in Luke 19.11-26.

has become a man of God with a story that impacts other guys for the better. He is helping these men find their path to recovery. For the first time in as long as he can remember, the recovering addict can hold his head high and say with assurance...

"He restores my soul;
He leads me in the paths of righteousness
For His name's sake."
Psalm 23.3 NKJV

423 Men offers real hope to hurting men.

7 MARITAL DISCLOSURE

If a married man working toward recovery in 423 Men is experiencing marital disharmony, he accepts responsibility to do his part to fix his marriage, or will die trying. Does that sound overly dramatic? It shouldn't, because that's what the Bible teaches:

"Husbands, love your wives, just as Christ loved the church and gave himself up for her..." Ephesians 5.25 NIV

Jesus died for the church and we are to love our wives in the same sacrificial way Christ loved the church; that is, to the death. I used to tell my wife, "I'd take a bullet for you." My promise to die never seemed to overly impress Adonica. "I'd rather have you take out the garbage once in a while." What my wife really wanted was for me to listen better and help more around the house. Not a very dazzling or manly job description. I'd rather get kudos for being a hero than for washing the dishes, but serving my wife unselfishly was God's way for me to die – die to self.

One day Adonica observed in my hearing, "There are clean clothes at the bottom of the stairs." I knew it was my job to listen to my wife, so I trotted right over to the steps leading to the second level of our home and confirmed what she told me, "Why yes, dear. There are clean clothes at the bottom of the stairs." I thought I had fulfilled my husbandly duty. I listened to and even affirmed my wife's statement. What she actually meant was, "Please find the clean clothes in the laundry basket at the foot of the stairs and take them up to the bedrooms." My first thought was, "Why didn't you just say so?" but I somehow understood the folly of that course of action. As dense as I was, I had to admit that even I knew the meaning of her words. In this instance, I deliberately missed an opportunity to love my wife "just as Christ loved the church and gave himself up for her." I was unwilling (at first) to die to self on her behalf. (I eventually took the laundry basket upstairs.)

It's occasionally good to revisit your marriage vows:

"I, _____,
take you, _____,
to be my wedded wife,
and I do promise before God and these witnesses,
to be your loving and faithful husband,
and to cherish you, in plenty and in want,
in joy and in sorrow, in sickness and in health,
for better or for worse, as long as we both shall live."

Do you feel differently today than you did on the day you first made this pledge? Visualize your woman whose "worth is far above jewels" (Proverbs 31.10 NAS) and quietly repeat these vows in your mind to her now. Have you fulfilled them, entirely, partially, or not at all? If you have been in pursuit of πορνεία at any time since your wedding day, or even since the first day of your engagement, then you have not entirely fulfilled your intended or actual vows to be a "loving and faithful husband." Unless you have already told her of your infractions, you have something to confess to your wife. Learning to love your marriage companion is a lifelong adventure, and part of the journey includes full disclosure.

Your wife should expect, and certainly deserves, singular and exclusive sexual devotion of the kind described by Solomon:

"Drink water from your own cistern,
And fresh water from your own well.
Should your springs be dispersed abroad,
Streams of water in the streets?
Let them be yours alone,
And not for strangers with you.

Let your fountain be blessed,
And rejoice in the wife of your youth.
As a loving hind and a graceful doe,
Let her breasts satisfy you at all times;
Be exhilarated always with her love. "
Proverbs 5.15-19 NASB

If, instead, you have chosen to "embrace the bosom of a foreigner" (Proverbs 5.20 NAS) bearing the name πορνεία, don't you think she deserves to know?

"Why be captivated, my son, by an adulteress?
Why embrace the bosom of another man's wife?
For a man's ways are in full view of the LORD,
  and He examines all his paths.
The evil deeds of a wicked man ensnare him;
His own iniquities will capture the wicked,
  the cords of his sin hold him fast.
He will die for lack of discipline,
  led astray by his own great folly. "
Proverbs 5.20-23 NIV 1984

Many men with sexually addictive behavior patterns try to keep their wives in the dark. "I can't tell my wife about my porn use because I don't want to hurt her" which more likely means, "I can't tell my wife about my porn use because I don't want *her* to hurt *me!*" You may have good reason to fear. "Hell hath no fury like a woman scorned."[37] As a husband, you have probably learned that your wife has the power to inflict pain, and your failure to disclose may be driven as much by your need for self-preservation than by a sincere desire to keep from causing grief to your "wedded wife." The charade will not last. Wives will eventually learn the truth for one simple reason… secrets don't work.

Occasionally, a woman will cooperate with her mate's

---

[37] Paraphrase of line by Zara in Act III, Scene VIII of *"The Mourning Bride"* (1697) by 17th century English playwright, William Congreve. The actual quotation is "Heaven has no rage like love to hatred turned, Nor hell as fury like a woman scorned."

misbehavior by choosing not to pry. Perhaps she is afraid to learn of the truth she suspects, but as she willingly closes her eyes to the facts, she involuntarily closes her heart to her "wedded husband." His dirty little secret is, "I use porn." Hers is, "I don't want to know," or worse, "I know and don't care." This unwholesome arrangement undermines their covenant of love to the detriment of both marriage partners.

My wife and I made an agreement early in our union... "No secrets." Adonica and I always believed this policy was in the best interest of our marital union, so I told her everything. I'm pretty sure she did the same. We kept no secrets.

There are no secrets with God. He sees all, and eventually, so does everyone else. Speaking on behalf of God, the prophet Jeremiah stated, "For I am closely watching you, and I see every sin. You cannot hope to hide from me" (Jeremiah 16.17 TLB). Secrecy is an illusion. To think otherwise is the porn addict's folly:

> *"He says to himself, 'God will never notice;*
> *He covers his face and never sees.'" Psalm 10.11 NIV 2011*

> *"The eye of the adulterer watches for dusk;*
> *he thinks, 'No eye will see me,'*
> *and he keeps his face concealed." Job 24.15 NIV*

Wouldn't it be better to proactively inform your wife of improprieties than reactively defend yourself when she learns of them? Jesus said, "For nothing is secret that will not be revealed, nor anything hidden that will not be known and come to light" (Luke 8.17 NKJV). Of this you may be assured... the person you are on the inside and the things you do in secret will someday be known by anyone who cares to know, including your wife.

> "Well you may throw your rock and hide your hand,
>   Workin' in the dark against your fellow man;
>   But as sure as God made black and white,
>   What's done in the dark will be brought to the light."[38]

---

[38] Johnny Cash *"God's Gonna Cut You Down"* from posthumous album *American V: A Hundred Highways*, released 2006.

Your Wife Cannot be Your Accountability Partner

Some guys tell me, "My wife is my accountability partner." Personally, I think that is a bad idea. Allow me to illustrate. Let's pretend your closest friend is a 'violence addict' with a particular affinity for stabbing people with a sharp knife. Periodically, he is overcome with blood-lust and thrusts a blade into your back. When you awake from surgery, your friend is at your bedside and ready to confess. "I'm so sorry I hurt you. Please forgive me. When you get out of the hospital, we will start all over and pretend this never happened. I know I have a problem, but I am trying to get help. I still love you. You are my best friend. Would you be my 'accountability partner'? Every time I feel the desire to stab you, I will confess and you can hold me accountable. If I stab you when you are not looking, I promise to quickly admit my sin and you can help me not to do that again. Agreed?"

I think you can see the foolishness of such an offer. You may not intend to hurt your wife, but your pursuit of πορνεία does exactly that. Unlike the members of your 423 Men group, she cannot remain 'arm's length' or objective. Your woman is bleeding emotionally because you betrayed her. She is not sure she can trust you. Her ears are deaf to your hollow assurances. She wants change, not promises. You must confess and fully disclose to your beloved if you intend to properly recover, but do not expect her to make you better. That's your job, not hers. Find followers of Jesus who, like you, struggle with sexual sin and take the recovery plunge with them.

Intimacy

All good marriages are characterized by emotional intimacy. You can't have intimacy without honesty. It takes courage to honestly confess your sexual past with an angry and hurt wife or fiancée, but the woman you promised to "cherish... as long as we both shall live" deserves to know who she married or who she plans to marry. At intake interviews, each prospective 423 Men member is instructed, "If married or engaged, we fully and honestly confess our history of sexual sin to our wives or fiancées. Initial disclosure of this kind should be made early in our recovery process after prayer, careful preparation, and wise counsel from our group leaders."[39] 423 Men recommends that each member disclose to his wife or fiancée only after becoming stabilized in his recovery so she may witness progress and have reason for hope in his continued sexual sobriety. However, we do not support the idea that a man may delay his confession for fear of "hurting" his wife or fiancée. He must not dawdle on this important step. Avoidance behavior kills significant relationships because it undermines trust. Procrastination is not consistent with a legitimate recovery plan because it will invariably provide an excuse for the addict to continue sinning sexually. Integrity and love demand that he confess to his wife soon after joining 423 Men, and if engaged, share his sexual history with his fiancée well before the wedding day.

It's easy to avoid honest confession with a wife, fiancée, or serious girlfriend and run instead into the arms (tentacles) of πορνεία. Your woman will expect change from you. She may not seem as gracious or understanding as the men in your recovery group. Your wife may even withhold sex after hearing of your past sexual exploits, not as a manipulative tool to force change in you, but simply because she's hurt. If you are not willing or able to protect her from the entry of this destructive sin into your relationship, then she must take action to keep herself emotionally and physically safe.

After disclosure, it continues to be your job to love, nurture, and cherish the woman God gave you. Your job description will include:

Demonstrate actions which back up your words.
Offer her patient and consistent reassurance.
Don't allow yourself to become defensive.
Listen quietly and don't try to "fix" or correct her.
Remain active in your sexual recovery plan and group.
Honestly share with her your progress in recovery.
Quickly confess when you fall below your sobriety line.
Implement a mutually agreed upon relapse prevention plan.
Regularly share your victories with her.
Always remind her of your undying devotion and love.

---

[39] Item 16 on *"Typical 423 Meeting"* included in the Appendix of this book.

Be a devoted follower of Jesus.
Encourage her to join a women's support group.[40]

Your wife is the woman of your dreams. She is the only woman for you. She alone is your standard of beauty. The 'other woman,' the so-called woman of your sexual fantasies, requires nothing from you, at first. She appears beautiful, understanding, warm, kind, sexy, and completely at your service, but her promise of fulfillment is wholly unnatural, phony, unreal, and demonic. She is πορνεία and nothing more than a skinny veneer for Satan himself. She 'disguises herself as an angel of light' and 'masquerades as a servant of righteousness' (see 2nd Corinthians 11.14-15 NAS, NIV). This "woman" will destroy you in the end.

"A woman came to meet him, dressed like a prostitute,[41] having a hidden agenda... Come, let's drink deeply of lovemaking until morning. Let's feast on each other's love!... She seduces him with her persistent pleading; she lures with her flattering talk. He follows her impulsively like an ox going to the slaughter, like a deer bounding toward a trap until an arrow pierces its liver, like a bird darting into a snare—he doesn't know it will cost him his life." Proverbs 7.10, 18, 21-23 HCSB

The most important step in establishing intimacy with your wife is to tell her the truth about your sexual history. Many men would prefer to sacrifice intimacy on the altar of concealment. They would rather keep secrets than face the marital fallout and discord their full disclosure would likely cause. A decision to hide pertinent sexual facts from your wife is a form of deceit which is neither

---

[40] Your beloved needs help too. It is crucial that your wife, girlfriend, or fiancée find support and get real answers from other women who have similarly suffered. Recovery programs like 423 Betrayal & Beyond are highly effective in helping a woman rebuild trust and find hope in the aftermath of the betrayal and brokenness caused by her man's pursuit of πορνεία. There she will find specific safety strategies, like the development of a RAP (Recovery Action Plan) which provides for impartial and manageable consequences to her man's sexual misconduct.

[41] The word "prostitute" used in Proverbs 7.10 of the Septuagint, the Greek translation of the Hebrew Scriptures (LXX) is πορνικόν, transliterated pornikón, a derivative of the word πορνεία.

respect-worthy of you nor respectful of her. A doctor does not cover an infected wound with a bandage and call it good. That's a quack, not a true practitioner. Rather, medical protocol demands that the doctor cause additional pain by further opening the wound, scouring the injury with disinfectant, and applying a proper bandage. Don't be a quack of a husband. Step into the fray. Open, clean, and heal the wound. Take a risk. Man of God, tell the truth and fix your failing marriage, or die trying.

The Hebrew meaning of the verb 'to know,' when applied to God, "is to have an intimate experiential knowledge of Him."[42] It is not surprising, then, that one of the variety of meanings for the same Hebrew word 'to know' is sexual intercourse.[43] God's design for sex was intended to be so much more than a physical act. To 'know' my wife in the biblical sense means to truly experience the wonder and remarkableness of who she is, and to strive to make myself known to her in a similar way. Secrets are banned in this sacred setting. Intimacy of this kind literally dispels shame.

"Adam and his wife were both naked, and they felt no shame."
Genesis 2.25 NIV 2011

Sex, then, is sacramental in the sense that it is a physical expression of true intimacy between husband and wife resulting in further impartation of God's grace to strengthen the union. Sex, of course, is not the main goal of marriage. Nakedness is an emotional concept long before it is a physical one. Great sex is not characterized by real nakedness, but by naked realness between a man and a woman in holy matrimony. The goal of marriage is intimacy and 'oneness' beautifully expressed in many acts of love, including the act of lovemaking.

---

[42] Yada' (to know) *Vine's Expository Dictionary of Biblical Words*, Thomas Nelson Publishers, 1985.

[43] יָדַע (to know, transliterated yada') is also used for sexual intercourse in the well-known euphemism "Adam knew Eve his wife" and its parallels (Genesis 4.1; 19.8; Numbers 31.17,35; Judges 11.39; 21:11; 1st Samuel 1.19; 1st Kings 1.4). From *Theological Wordbook of the Old Testament*, The Moody Bible Institute of Chicago, 1980.

"For this cause a man shall leave his father and his mother, and shall cleave to his wife; and they shall become one flesh." Genesis 2.24 NASB

In the context of 423 Men, the true "one flesh" union begins with a man's decision to become fully transparent, authentic, and honest with his wife. Honesty is not a game. It is a matter of life and death for the marital union. "Full disclosure," you say, "will kill my marriage, if she doesn't kill me first." If that is true, then your marriage is already dead and it's your job to bring it back to life. Start by telling her the truth about who you are: what you've done and why you did it. She may not take it well, so you need to stay closely connected to your 423 Men group. You will receive enough reinforcement from your brothers in recovery to make up for any emotional support shortage you may be forced to endure at home.

Show courage and humility. Trust Jesus, and trust your wife. I have personally witnessed more than one "wife of noble character" (Proverbs 31.10 NIV) stick by her wedding vows and her fallen man when everyone else advised her to "dump him" and tell him "goodbye for good." The tenacity of these faithful wives was staggering to me. Your wife may be more resilient and ready to fight for your relationship than you expect (or than she initially led you to believe). While she may feel crushed by your sin, your spouse may also feel, for the first time, relief and validation. I have heard women say, after their husbands' confession, "I always knew something was wrong. I thought I was going crazy. Now, at least, I know it's not me. His sin is finally out in the open. We can get help and build up our marriage from here." Tell your wife "the truth, the whole truth, and nothing but the truth." Honesty is the foundation of intimacy and should define your marriage from this point forward.

One word of caution... don't disclose alone. It is critical that you first receive wise counsel from your 423 Men leaders and, if possible, in conjunction with advice from women leaders in 423 Betrayal & Beyond. They will assist you in forming the right approach and in selecting the proper timing for your confession. Your disclosure is not for your catharsis. It is for your wife's sense of well-being and healing. If your disclosure is made haphazardly without thoughtful prayer, careful preparation, and wise counsel, you could cause more damage than good.

"Stand firm in the faith, act like men, be strong. Let all that you do be done in love" (1ˢᵗ Corinthians 16.13-14 NAS). Like Jesus who called Lazarus from the tomb days after his death (John 11.43), boldly cry out to God for the resurrection of your dying marriage.

Guilt-Free Sex

Sex may not be the best thing in the world, but *guilt-free sex* must certainly be close to the top of the list. Frequent sex between a happily married man and woman is about as good as it gets. It's a slice of heaven on earth. I once saw a wedding greeting card with an illustration of a couple leaping for joy, champagne in hand. The front of the card read, *"Enjoy your wedding day, but try to keep in mind that marriage isn't just two people prancing around naked and engaging in all sorts of uncivilized behavior..."* Opening the card, *"...although that's certainly something to aim for."* I laughed out loud (LOL) in hearty agreement.

Sexual intercourse, as God designed it, is the culmination of the most intimate, energizing, positive, joy-filled, idyllic expression of romantic love this world has to offer. No human could have invented sex. It's far too remarkable. It transcends the farthest regions of all carnal imagination.

> *"There are three things that are too wonderful for me,*
> *four that I do not understand:*
> *the way of an eagle in the sky,*
> *the way of a snake on a rock,*
> *the way of a ship in the sea,*
> *and the way of a man with a woman."*
> Proverbs 30.18-19 NET

Sex is a divine gift. Why would anyone, after tasting Eden's pure pleasure, settle for a counterfeit replica of the real thing? By comparison to God's plan for sex, πορνεία offers nothing. Solo-sex with computerized images of women is cheap and easy but, of course, you get what you pay for. Cheap sex is any sex costing a man less than a lifelong commitment of fidelity in marriage with one woman. Paradoxically, it leaves him unsatisfied and hungry for more of the same. The cheap sex habit becomes addictive and tends to escalate because it will not satisfy. Just as John Mayer said (see Chapter 4), "Twenty seconds ago you thought that photo was the hottest thing you ever saw, but you throw it back and continue your shot hunt…"

If you are not experiencing great sex God's way, do your level best to find it in the arms of a loving wife whom you commit to cherish "as long as you both shall live."

"He who finds a wife finds a good thing, and obtains favor from the LORD." Proverbs 18.22 NKJV

In the meantime, trust Him who has your best intentions at heart. God does not promise an unlimited supply of guilt-free sex throughout life. If you now have it, rejoice. If you don't, trust God who Himself said, "It is not good for the man to be alone. I will make a helper suitable for him" (Genesis 2.18 NIV). Jesus is able to help you find the right woman perfectly suited for you, and during seasons of singleness, He will impart the grace you need to patiently wait.

God proved His love for me with the gift of marriage to an amazing wife. He granted me two decades of companionship, intimacy, love, and unbridled passion with the woman of my dreams. Whatever price I paid to pursue, court, nurture, and keep this woman was, in my estimation, wholly inadequate. She was worth much, much more than my highest and best efforts. Adonica was a divine gift, freely bestowed and wholly unmerited. She satisfied me in every way a woman can possibly satisfy a man. I did not deserve her. She knew every detail of my sexual history, and still she fully accepted me. Adonica loved and respected me in spite of myself. This woman was to me tangible evidence of God's transcendent mercy. Now she is in heaven, yet her example of godliness leaves me forever convinced of God's goodness. I could never replace her, nor will I ever try. I may remarry, but if I do not, Adonica's love will last me for the rest of my life on earth. It will carry me until the day I see her again.

I no longer need πορνεία. Neither do you.

8 THE BATTLE FOR EMOTIONAL SURVIVAL

We are all engaged in a battle for emotional survival. There are causalities in this battle. People get hurt. Painful memories clutter the deserted battlefields of our wounded souls. Internal pain bubbles to the surface of our awareness, reminding us of our own neediness and propelling us in the pursuit of πορνεία. Our addiction presents itself as a quick and easy 'fix' for broken relationships, never-met needs, and childhood traumas. The 'fix,' of course, fixes nothing because it focuses itself on self, and not others. When will I realize I am not alone in the battle? My opponents are also fighting for their emotional survival. Perhaps the pursuit of my own healing is incidental to a higher objective – that of helping others do the same, even when I am estranged from those who need my help and healing touch. Who knows? I may need them as much as they need me. Perhaps there is a reason Jesus commanded me to "make friends quickly with [my] opponent."

> *"If therefore you are presenting your offering at the altar, and there remember that your brother has something against you, leave your offering there before the altar, and go your way; first be reconciled to your brother, and then come and present your offering. Make friends quickly with your opponent..."* Jesus, Matthew 5.23-25a NASB

If the pain caused by broken relationships is an impetus for sexual addiction, does it not stand to reason that the healing of these relationships can reverse that trend? Resolution of conflicts with difficult people, then, becomes central to the goals of recovery. We can overcome sexual sin, but we cannot do it alone. We need reconciliation as much for our benefit as for those we may have once wished to never see again.

Didn't our mothers teach us, "There are two sides to every argument"? Forgiveness not only helps opposing factions to see the *other* side, but can enable adversarial people to get on the *same* side of the battle. We're in this human struggle together. We need each other. Our antagonists are also fighting for their emotional survival... just like we are.

What if we extended an olive branch?

> *"Blessed are the peacemakers, for they will be called children of God."* Jesus, Matthew 5.9 NIV 2011

What if we chose to get along with hard-to-get-along-with people?

> *"Live in harmony with one another."* Romans 12.16a NIV

What if we sincerely tried to help those who offended us?

> *"If your enemy is hungry, feed him; if he is thirsty, give him something to drink."* Romans 12.20 NIV, quoting Proverbs 25.21

What if we showed sincere affection to all?

> *"Greet one another with a holy kiss."* Romans 16.16 NIV

What if we tried to forgive those who hurt us?

> *"And Jesus said, 'Father, forgive them, for they know not what they do.'"* Luke 23.34 ESV

Forgiveness offers hope for peace in the battle for emotional survival. The act of forgiveness is a powerful antidote for the sickness of sexual addiction.

Dad and Me

My dad and I had a rough time growing up together. Dad was a Lieutenant Colonel when he retired from the United States Air Force, having spent the majority of his career in the cockpit training pilots. For a short time, Dad required my brother and me to stand at attention and answer all questions with "Yes, Sir" or "No, Sir." Mom finally had enough and overrode Sir Dad. "They're children, Gil, not cadets."

I was the oldest of three and, as a teenager, rebelled against Dad's heavy handed, militaristic approach to child rearing. I often felt berated by my father and, after one particularly demeaning experience, I slammed my bedroom door and took a baseball bat from my closet. I swore to myself, "If he comes into my room, I'll kill him. I hate him."

I sought solace in the comfort of sexual fantasies. What my adolescent brain could not grasp at the time was that Dad and I were in this turmoil together. While I was fighting my dad, he was fighting his demons from past violent encounters with his own father. When I was in hot pursuit of πορνεία to relieve my emotional pain, so was Dad. My father bought pornography, used it, and then hid it. I found his stash, used it, and then put it back where I found it. Dad and I weren't so different, were we? It did not occur to me until many years later, that I was not the only one caught in the cycle of shame in my family of origin. So was Dad. We were on parallel paths, fighting (and losing) the very same battle with sexual addiction. I now wonder…

What if Dad caught me with one of his dirty magazines? Could that have caused a confrontation that might have resulted in healing for both of us?

Did Mom know Dad hid pornographic magazines? If she did, why did she allow it? Didn't she care? Was she able to care?

Did Dad know I was sneaking peeks at his *Playboy's*? If he did, why did he allow it? Didn't he care? Was he able to care?

Our suffering was somehow linked, even complementary. It fit together like a psychological jig-saw puzzle. If Dad suffered, so would I. If he beat his demons, so would I. We were in the battle for emotional survival together.

I learned that my paternal grandfather was a drunk and a wife beater. My dad was once a boy like me, trapped in the chaos and dysfunction of his family of origin. Years later, for reasons I still cannot fully comprehend, my dad was compelled to take out his father-hatred on his longhaired, oldest son. We were both just trying to survive. What neither one of us comprehended was that my emotional survival meant his, and his meant mine.

Dad did not enter my room that day, and I never took a swing at him with a wooden bat. However, more fist fights would follow during my high school years.

Once my mother tried to break up one of our more violent brawls. I took a swing at Dad. He ducked and my punch landed on Mom's jaw. "Look what you did to my wife," he screamed, and upped the intensity of the beating. The next day I proudly showed off my facial bruising to awestruck buddies. It was a different era then, but I suspect I was physically abused in ways most of my friends were not.

When I was in first grade we lived in Greenville, Mississippi. Mom was out of town with my baby sister attending Grandpa's funeral. My dad was home alone, taking care of my younger brother, Rick, and me. During breakfast one morning, I dropped a gallon jar of milk spreading white liquid and shattered glass all over the kitchen floor. Dad lost control of himself, and with arms flailing, screamed, "God damn it! God damn it." Dad was bigger than life, and Rick and I were just little squirts. We were pretty frightened.

About forty years later, I invited my father out for breakfast. I was fairly new in my recovery from sexual addiction. We sat in a McDonald's restaurant in Beaverton, Oregon, and I reminded him of the spilled milk incident. He well remembered the event and many other times he lost his temper and became physically or verbally abusive with Rick and me. He humbly expressed his sorrow for the way he raised us. Dad explained that those memories were kept locked up in a deep, black vault of pain in his heart. He did not like to think about them. I suggested we go to that dark place, and I reminded my dad that we were in this struggle together. His black hole of regret was my black hole of abuse. His way out was to plunge into the darkness and acknowledge his sin. My way out was to take the plunge with him and offer forgiveness. God forgave him and so did I. I suggested we could visit these unhappy times together with Jesus, and perhaps Dad could learn to forgive himself. Together we wept in public over coffee and Egg McMuffins. Dad found peace. He embraced his emotional pain and helped me do the same. We helped each other.

Dad was not all bad. He was a soldier. My father would have taken a bullet and given his life, without question, to protect me. He did not know how to express his love any better than to fulfill his duty as a military man. My father loved me the best he knew how. He simply was not prepared for a boy like me with a mind of his own. We clashed hard, but reconciled well. I forgave him. I had to for my own emotional wellbeing. There was no other way. Our reconciliation saved him, and it saved me as well. Only Jesus could have accomplished such a miracle of redemption. Dad and I remained fast friends until he died on July 23rd, 2005. I cried again at his funeral, and still do occasionally, when I consider the loss of this imperfect but good man who helped, in his broken way, to shape me into the decent man I am today.

Emotional pain does not go away. The intensity may lessen in time, but it will never disappear. I still think about my childhood from time to time. Some of these memories make me smile and feel warm all over. Others hurt, still, but I am learning to forgive myself and those who contributed to my suffering. When I forgave my dad, I set both myself and Dad free. When my father willingly participated in my journey of healing, he set himself and me free. I'm not sure how this worked, I just know that it did. The emotional pain Dad and I carried defined us and, at the point of reconciliation, became the best part of our Jesus story together.

Before Dad died, I invited him to attend a retreat where I was the featured speaker. With a little nudge from my mom, "Go ahead, Gil; go to the retreat with your son," he chose to attend. I shall never forget the joy and peace that washed over me when I beheld from the podium my own father weep as I spoke about the love we found and then shared together. Our redemption was mutually contagious and complete. It took a generation of time to make our peace, but we did, together. Thankfully, we realized, before it was too late, that we were on the same side in the battle for emotional survival.

Jacob and Esau

Jacob was not ready to face his brother. Twenty years earlier he had swindled Esau out of his birthright and blessing. "Esau bore a grudge against Jacob" and promised, "I will kill my brother" (Genesis 27.41 NAS). Their mother, Rebekah, warned Jacob and he fled for his life. Rebekah was shockingly naïve, thinking Esau would soon be done with his rage.

"Flee at once to my brother Laban in Haran. Stay with him for a while until your brother's fury subsides. When your brother is no longer angry with you and forgets what you did to him, I'll send word for you to come back from there." Genesis 27.43-45 NIV

Jacob fled, but Esau would not forgive Jacob anytime soon. Rebekah's plan backfired because she way underestimated the intensity of Esau's emotional pain. 'He'll get over it' was not to be in her probable lifetime. Jacob spent twenty years in Haran and there is no biblical record of Rebekah's death or reunion with Jacob. While rabbinical opinions vary on this point, Rebekah probably never saw her favored son again. It seems safe to suggest that Rebekah would not realize her plan to reunite the boys into one happy family.

The night before the brothers were to meet again, Jacob was overcome by fear. It was time to face the music and pay for his crimes against Esau. He couldn't sleep and wrestled with an angel of God all night long. At daybreak, the angel told him, "Your name will no longer be Jacob, but Israel, because you have struggled with God and humans and have overcome," (Genesis 32.28 NIV 2011). The next morning, when Jacob and Esau met for the first time in many, many years...

"Esau ran to meet Jacob and embraced him; threw his arms around his neck and kissed him, and they wept." Genesis 33.4 NAS

The story ends well, but Jacob's encounter with God did not leave him unscathed.

"The sun rose above him..., and he was limping because of his hip." Genesis 32.31 NIV

Jacob walked with a limp for the rest of his life, which was representative of the pain he had to suffer to become the man he was destined to be – Israel, father of the twelve tribes of the Hebrew nation.

At first glance, this story seems to be primarily about Jacob, but the account of father Israel is actually an intertwining narrative about two brothers, Jacob and Esau. Both of these men were fighting for their emotional survival. What they did not know, at the onset of their conflict, was that they were in this struggle together. The brothers contending for family dominance were actually on the same side of the battle.

After learning of Jacob's scam, Esau begged his father Isaac for a second blessing. "'Do you have only one blessing, my father? Bless me too, my father!' Then Esau wept aloud" (Genesis 27.38 NIV). Isaac recanted and gave his first son what appears to be a cut-rate benediction:

> *"Your dwelling will be*
> *   away from the earth's richness,*
> *   away from the dew from heaven above.*
> *You will live by the sword*
> *   and you will serve your brother.*
> *But when you grow restless,*
> *   you will throw his yoke*
> *   from off your neck."*
> Genesis 27.39-40 NIV

Esau's supposed "blessing" fascinates me. It appears to contain three components:

1. Esau would be less of a farmer, and more of a hunter "away from the earth's richness."

2. Esau would have a violent nature and "live by the sword."

3. Esau would "serve [his] brother" until he would finally "grow restless" and "throw [Jacob's] yoke from off his neck."

How shall we interpret this blessing? To my knowledge, Esau did not "serve" Jacob, or *did* he? Could the "grudge" he bore and the desire to "kill" his brother be, in fact, the service he was forced to render? Was Esau in bondage for twenty years to his own bitterness against the man who stole his fortune?

Jacob sent messengers to inform his twin of his near arrival, appealing to what he hoped would be Esau's good nature. "I have sent these messengers to inform my lord of my coming, hoping that you will be friendly to me" (Genesis 32.5 NLT). The emissaries returned with bad news.

> *"After delivering the message, the messengers returned to Jacob and reported, 'We met your brother, Esau, and he is already on his way to meet you—with an army of 400 men!' Jacob was terrified at the news."* Genesis 32.6-7 NLT

"An army of 400 men" suggests no change in Esau's two-decade-old vendetta to slay Jacob.

I cannot prove the following assertion, but I believe Esau fulfilled and received his father's blessing when he finally rid himself of "the yoke" of bitterness. The rightful heir of Isaac's blessings 'threw the yoke from off his neck' on the day and in the precise instance he came face to face with his estranged brother. Something good snapped in Esau's brain. He finally "grew restless" of harboring resentment. He laid aside his "grudge," overcame his "fury," threw down his "sword," and forgave his brother. Jacob and Esau were in a battle for emotional survival together. Esau had to forgive Jacob. It was the only way to finally possess the blessing of Isaac. Jacob's struggle for mercy was Esau's struggle to forgive. Each man set the other free on the day they reconciled, embraced, kissed, and wept.

An Axe to Grind and a Hatchet to Bury

None of us get through life without emotional scrapes and bruises. These wounds are often deep and painful. We can always find someone else to blame for our suffering, even when we are actually, or at least partially, responsible.

The term 'axe to grind' traces its probable etymology to one or two 18th century statesmen from Pennsylvania, Benjamin Franklin and Charles Miner. While the phrase can mean the possession of a hidden agenda, ulterior motive, or pet subject, I favor the arguably more common usage of bearing a grudge or harboring a grievance. This meaning originates from the gruesome idea of sharpening an axe on a grinding wheel, with the intent to get revenge by maiming or killing the individual causing our grief. Used metaphorically, the saying indicates a wishing of harm on the person who wronged us. This unhealthy desire feeds our addictive tendency by justifying our bad choices. "She's the reason I am driven to drink (look at porn, lose my temper, kick the dog, gamble too much, use cocaine, spend money I don't have, etc.).

You may well have been harmed by others. You may be a victim of another's abuse or negligence. I am not suggesting you were not mistreated, but only that judgment, retribution, and vengeance toward the person causing the injustice is not yours to render, even in the privacy of your thought life.

> *"Do not take revenge, my dear friends, but leave room for God's wrath, for it is written: 'It is mine to avenge; I will repay,' says the Lord... Do not be overcome by evil, but overcome evil with good."*
> Romans 12.19, 21 NIV 2011, quoting Deuteronomy 32.35

Having 'an axe to grind' is a shallow, hollow, and one-dimensional way of thinking. Left alone to fester, your 'axe' will evolve into full-fledged resentment. The Bible refers to this progression as a "root of bitterness" which "springs up and causes trouble, and by it many become defiled" (Hebrews 12.15b ESV). According to the prophet Ezekiel, nothing earns the disfavor of God more quickly than harboring "an ancient hostility," an "age-old grudge," a "cherished perpetual enmity," or a "long-standing hatred," (see Ezekiel 35.5 in NIV, *The Message*, ESV, and CJB versions of the Bible).

Your "ancient hostility" presumes that you are the central figure in any conflict you experience, when, in fact, the drama may include many actors, some of whom played in scenes of which you were never a part. Your 'trauma drama' is actually multi-dimensional: the players who caused you pain have their own story and you were only incidentally related. Thoughtful consideration of the issues, conflicts, trauma, and stressors which may have prompted your adversary's bad behavior can help to soften your attitude and pave the way for forgiveness. Emotional pain, especially when it can be traced to a perpetrator, affords you with an opportunity to get outside of yourself, connect with Christ, and view the situation from His perspective. Eugene Peterson's paraphrase of Colossians 3.1-2 in *The Message* version of the Bible perfectly illustrates our responsibility to interpret harsh and painful realities from heaven's vantage point:

> *"So if you're serious about living this new resurrection life with Christ, act like it. Pursue the things over which Christ presides. Don't shuffle along, eyes to the ground, absorbed with the things right in front of you. Look up, and be alert to what is going on around Christ — that's where the action is. See things from his perspective."*

If you have 'an axe to grind,' then you also have a hatchet to bury; that is, an occasion to make peace with those who are the source of your emotional pain.

The term 'bury the hatchet' hearkens back to a native American ritual of burying two tomahawks, one by each feuding tribe, as a ceremonial gesture of peace and the cessation of war.

Bury the axe you are grinding! You no longer need to "shuffle along, eyes to the ground, absorbed" in fantasies of personal victimization and revenge. It's time to look up and realize your perceived enemy is just like you, engaged in a battle for emotional survival. Bitterness is a bad dream and forgiveness awakens you to the possibility of finding common ground with your opponent. Do not underestimate the power of forgiveness in breaking the stranglehold of addiction.

The offering of forgiveness hurts, at first, like the bearing of a cross:

"If anyone wishes to come after Me, he must deny himself, and take up his cross daily and follow Me. For whoever wishes to save his life will lose it, but whoever loses his life for My sake, he is the one who will save it." Luke 9.23-24 NASU

Nothing causes a more intense sense of the loss of self than the naturally distasteful decision to let go of a long-held grudge, a long-nurtured hostility, or a long-cherished vendetta. Yet nothing provides a more immediate sense of relief and peace, or more closely aligns with Jesus' call to 'lose your life, take up your cross daily, and follow Him,' than the supernaturally empowering decision to pardon others of the wrongs they have committed against you.

"And forgive us our debts,
As we forgive our debtors."
Jesus, Matthew 6.12 NKJV

Your axe to grind is your hatchet to bury. Forgive and be set free.

Relational Log Jams

Forgiveness releases the miraculous power of God's Spirit to do the impossible. Imagine your difficult relationships as a log jam. How do you loosen the jam? You can step out into the middle of the river and remove one log at a time. However, log picking your relationships is a very dangerous endeavor and discouraged by Jesus Himself:

"And why worry about a speck in your friend's eye when you have a log in your own? How can you think of saying to your friend, 'Let me help you get rid of that speck in your eye,' when you can't see past the log in your own eye? Hypocrite! First get rid of the log in your own eye; then you will see well enough to

deal with the speck in your friend's eye. " Matthew 7.3-5 NLT

There is another, equally as damaging option... dynamite! That will definitely end, but never fixes, a relational log jam. The dynamite solution causes irreversible damage. When you utter what you'll soon regret, burn a bridge, hit below the belt, betray a friend, or offend anyone with hurtful words, your relationship is over, probably for good.

> *"It is harder to win back the friendship of an offended brother than to capture a fortified city. His anger shuts you out like iron bars. "* Proverbs 18.19 TLB

There is a better way; a safer and more redemptive alternative to log picking (trying to change people) or dynamite (ending relationships with people you cannot change). If you raise the level of the river the logs will simply float downstream. Forgiveness elevates the water level in hard interactions, making it possible for the logs in everyone's eyes to float gently away. Forgiveness unleashes the power of God and releases the rivers of living water in an addict's soul. Bitterness and resentment, petty differences of opinion, minor conflicts, and longstanding hostilities are not the only logs that get washed downstream. For reasons I cannot explain, πορνεία sometimes goes along for the ride. Your decision to forgive can break the stronghold of sexual addiction in your life.

> *"If it is possible, as far as it depends on you, live at peace with everyone. "* Romans 12.18 NIV

Your recovery is not just about you. It's about you and the people God placed in your life. Remind yourself often that others are engaged in their own battles for survival. Try to love and understand them. Nurture a spirit of compassion and empathy toward problem people. Trust Jesus and be a peacemaker. Forgive your adversaries, for in so doing, you are reinforcing your defense against the spirit of πορνεία and building hope for peace in your own battle for emotional survival.

9 EMBRACE THE DARKNESS

I began the second chapter of this book with a dirty four-letter word... P – A – I – N and stated, "We all carry some of it, at our core." Pain has a purpose, although it's often hard to fathom. Addicts are skilled at pain avoidance, but while it may come as a surprise to most people trapped in sexual addiction, facing your pain will not kill you. A little self-denial may feel like a fate worse than death, but it's not. In fact, choosing to feel the painful reality of what's inside of you, rather than clamoring for your sex drug, only makes you stronger. The more you *do* endure, the more you *can* endure. Jesus will never forsake you. He will always be there, holding you close at every step of the journey, in the midst of even the most horrific of personal traumas.

Emotional hurt will be your constant companion, or at least a regular visitor. Suffering occurs before, during, and after your recovery from sexual addiction. Pain doesn't go away. Your healing is not the eradication of pain, but rather its acceptance; or better stated, its absorption. It changes you for the better, if you let it. Your hurt, distress, sorrow, disappointment, and grief are permanently embedded in your life and voice. Underlying negative emotions shape your character and your message. If you choose to suffer redemptively; that is, to suffer with hope and a determination to learn from your trauma, you will develop into the man God destined you to become. Redemptive suffering creates within you the potential of leaving this world a better place than you found it. Your life matters. Suffering without hope inevitably leads to despair and relapse. Learning to properly identify and learn from, even embrace emotional pain, is your pathway to significance in God's kingdom.

"Pain handled in God's way produces a turning from sin to God which leads to salvation, and there is nothing to regret in that! But pain handled in the world's way produces only death. For just look at what handling the pain God's way produced in you! What earnest diligence, what eagerness to clear yourselves, what indignation, what fear, what longing, what zeal, what readiness to put things right! In everything you have proved yourselves blameless... " 2nd Corinthians 7.10-11 CJB

Suffering is a part of life, everybody's life. The guy who is active in his addiction is not unique. He has no more justification for sin than anyone else. Two points should be made here:

1. Fearless exploration of the underlying reasons for our addictive behavior is essential to the recovery process. Knowledge of the emotional pain we are trying to alleviate by the use of our destructive sexual activity will assist us on our journey toward healing.

2. Discovery of the underlying causes of our addictive patterns does not grant us permission to continue the sinful behavior. We cannot legitimately use emotional pain as an excuse for our addictions.

According to Jesus, for example, "Anyone who looks at a woman lustfully has already committed adultery with her in his heart," (Matthew 5.28 NIV). The man who commits "adultery... in his heart" might correctly state, "I sexualized the woman in my mind because I was stressed at work and looking for a release from my anxiety." This observation demonstrates good awareness and significant progress toward recovery, but it is not a defense for addictive behavior. He still committed "adultery... in his heart" and cannot rightly claim, "It was permissible for me to sexualize the woman in my mind because I was stressed at work and needed a release for my anxiety." The former statement is a legitimate answer to the right question, "Why did I act out sexually?" and hopefully leads to further self-revelation and active steps toward healthy sexuality, including the choice to suffer redemptively rather than medicate with sex. The latter derives its conclusion from a spirit of entitlement and uses stress and anxiety as an excuse in the pursuit of πορνεία.

Suffering Temptation

As a man progresses in recovery, he will learn about himself and discover the stressors, triggers, and traumatic events which historically led to his addictive lifestyle. This knowledge alone is not enough to achieve sobriety. The man caught in the trap of sexual addiction can know the reasons for his sin, and still want it. He must transition beyond self-awareness to battle readiness.

> *"Put on the full armor of God, so that you can take your stand against the devil's schemes. For our struggle is not against flesh and blood, but against the rulers, against the authorities, against the powers of this dark world and against the spiritual forces of evil in the heavenly realms. Therefore put on the full armor of God, so that when the day of evil comes, you may be able to stand your ground, and after you have done everything, to stand."* Ephesians 6.11-13 NIV

The addict must learn to accept the reality of the war being waged against his soul and the demonic nature of πορνεία's power. With the help of Jesus and his brothers in recovery, he can face, and even "overwhelmingly conquer" his demon (Romans 8.37 NAS). The recovering sex addict will eventually climb the mountain of self-discovery. By the time he reaches the summit, he will have gathered enough strength and confidence to take the next step. He is ready to do what he never before could do. It is all that he has left to do… take a stand and emphatically say "No!" to sexual addiction. He renounces his "secret and shameful ways" (2nd Corinthians 4.2a NIV) and makes "a covenant with [his] eyes not to look with lust at a young woman" (Job 31.1 NLT). The follower of Jesus dons "the full armor of God" so that, having "done everything," he may stand his ground against πορνεία's satanic assault. Standing up to your addiction is not easy; in fact, it's unequivocally frightening, even for a true man of God, but that's what men of God do. They gather the courage and humility to say (and mean), "Enough is enough!" I would be seriously remiss if I did not include a section in this book about the suffering which results from an active decision to resist temptation.

We're told that God is faithful and provides a way of escape to every temptation thrown our way.

"The temptations in your life are no different from what others experience. And God is faithful. He will not allow the temptation to be more than you can stand. When you are tempted, he will show you a way out so that you can endure."
1st Corinthians 10.13 NLT

That's good news for addicts everywhere, except for one little thing... the escape route God offers us comes with a price, the price of pain. "He will show you a way out so you can endure." I'd like "a way out" without the "endure" part. I'd prefer to be magically transported to a happy place where all bad things (including sexual temptations and painful memories) disappear like wisps of vapor on a breezy day. I long for the Garden of Eden without that pesky and tempting "tree of the knowledge of good and evil" (Genesis 2.17 NIV). I want an easy life with no hardships, where temptations instantly vanish at my command and without my slightest effort. Instead, I am cast into my own Garden of Gethsemane where life is characterized by struggle. I crave and grasp at what I cannot have, search for rationalizations, combat a spirit of entitlement, weep for my losses, feel the frailty of my humanness, bear the pain of my own making, second guess myself and God, wrestle with God, wrestle with my conscience, occasionally cave under the pressure of temptation, ask forgiveness as necessary, frequently remain steadfast, often stand in faith and walk in the Spirit, then falter and fight some more. The good news, and perhaps an indicator of maturity, is that my struggle is a little less intense now than it was in earlier years. The up and down swings are not as extreme. I am stabilizing and yet, while I am more receptive to the grace of God in the face of temptation than I was early in my recovery, the struggle and pain remain.

How can I choose God's "way out" of temptation without suffering? The answer is, I can't. "God is faithful," but His 'getaway plan' always includes suffering. It would have cost Adam and Eve something substantial to say "no" to the serpent's attractive offer. Refusing to partake of the "fruit from the tree that is in the middle of the garden" (Genesis 3.3 NIV) would have come with a price, if the first couple had chosen to pay it. The price was emotional pain, and the cost was too high. Adam and Eve did not choose to suffer the pain, and neither do we. But endurance and emotional pain go together. Resisting temptation is sacramental in nature and a form of redemptive suffering during which God bestows grace to remain firm and stand tall with dignity and in faith.

'Fleeing πορνεία' is a race in the opposite direction of sin. This race requires every ounce of endurance we can muster. It hurts, but it won't kill us. We can endure more than we think we can. We are not alone. Jesus and our brothers in recovery are running by our side, as we are running by theirs. Jesus fully understands our plight by virtue of His own humanity and personal experience of suffering. He "was led up by the Spirit into the wilderness to be tempted by the devil" (Matthew 4.1 NAS). Christ pushed back on the devil's attack, which, of course, qualified Him as one supremely able to identify with our painful predicament for time eternal.

> *"For this reason he* [Jesus Christ] *had to be made like his brothers in every way, in order that he might become a merciful and faithful high priest in service to God, and that he might make atonement for the sins of the people. Because he himself suffered when he was tempted, he is able to help those who are being tempted."* Hebrews 2.17-18 NIV 1984

Pride and fear keep the addict stuck in the cycle of shame. Addiction is the way an addict finds relief from emotional pain. It works, but not for long. Addiction is slow suicide. It's the path of Judas and leads to destruction. Recovery takes courage and humility. When a man shows the guts and humbleness of heart necessary to enter a recovery program like 423 Men, he is met with honor and respect. He is affirmed as a good man, not denounced as a weirdo or pervert. We remain sympathetic to his dilemma because

Jesus does. "We do not have a high priest who cannot sympathize with our weaknesses, but One who has been tempted in all things as we are, yet without sin" (Hebrews 4.15 NAS). If Jesus is sympathetic toward men with weaknesses, then who am I to allow an unsympathetic attitude toward anyone creep into my heart?

Temptation is common to all people, including Jesus. Christ is sympathetic because He, better than anyone else, understands the powerful attraction of sin. Jesus knew what it was like to suffer the temptation to sexualize women. Does it sound sacrilegious to suggest that the Lord was tempted to explore what lay forbidden under the skirts of pretty Galilean girls? It shouldn't. Unlike most men, Jesus did not succumb to the spirit of πορνεία, but to claim He did not suffer its temptation, would be to deny the straightforward biblical truth that Jesus was "tempted in all things as we are."

On the threshold of His ultimate hour of suffering, Jesus was offered "wine to drink, mingled with gall" (Matthew 27.34 RSV, see also parallel verse Mark 15.23). According to most commentators, this tonic was a crude narcotic intended to deaden the pain of Christ's crucifixion offered by merciful onlookers.[44] The Lord's refusal to partake after tasting the potion may be the recovering addict's greatest point of connection with Jesus. Our Savior's choice to embrace the full brunt of His pain, rather than to medicate it, is the supreme example of redemptive suffering and may provide hope to the addict who must also find the internal strength to say "no" to his drug of choice and choose to suffer instead.

<u>Chasing the Setting Sun</u>

After I lost Adonica, I read a fair number of books on grief. *A Grace Disguised* by Jerry Sittser spoke to me more profoundly than

---

[44] "...they offered him wine mingled with gall. This was a kind of stupefying liquor, a strong narcotic, made of the sour wine of the country, mingled with bitter herbs, and mercifully administered to dull the sense of pain. This was offered before the actual crucifixion took place... *But he received it not.* He would not seek alleviation of the agonies of the crucifixion by any drugged potion which might render him insensible. He would bear the full burden consciously" (*The Pulpit Commentary*, Spence and Exell, Funk & Wagnalls Co., 1880).

any other book I have read in the past few years. I highly recommend Dr. Sittser's book for everyone who has or will suffer loss, which, of course, is my way of saying, "I highly recommend Dr. Sittser's for everyone, *period*." The author's personal experience with grief made him instantly credible to me. About twenty years ago, Jerry lost his wife, daughter, and mother in the same car accident. He watched three precious family members die on the street after a drunk driver jumped the median and crashed head on into the vehicle Jerry was driving.

After reading *A Grace Disguised* I was compelled to meet the author to discuss the loss of my beautiful wife. I instinctively knew he would understand, and he did. I drove many hours to Dr. Sittser's hometown and poured out my broken heart over shared cups of coffee. He imparted great hope, but explained, given my love for Adonica, I would never "get over" my late wife. I could not simply "get past" my grief. Instead, I now had an opportunity to allow the pain of grief to change me. I could choose to suffer redemptively. My sorrow was real and it still is. I could not run from, dodge, or medicate it. I had to absorb it. I would forever be the man who lost his dear wife to cancer. Nothing could ever change that reality.

Jerry made several other observations which I shall always treasure:

Adonica was a gift God gave me for two decades. I must hold all gifts in an open-handed way.

Being a single parent to Robert and Rachel, my youngest children who are still at home, is also God's gift to me. I am incredibly privileged to be their dad.

As a grandparent, I have the joy and honor of helping my grown children "normalize" their parenting experiences. I get to purely "delight" in my grandkids.

I can be single, for the rest of my life, if that is God's will for me. He is enough.

Adonica was a beautiful and mighty, now fallen, tree. Her tree stump remains and continues to sustain beautiful life all around it.

After the death of his dear family members, Jerry described his loss in *A Grace Disguised.*

"Never have I experienced such anguish and emptiness. It was my first encounter with existential darkness, though it would not be my last.

"I had a kind of waking dream shortly after that, caused, I am sure, by that initial experience with darkness. I dreamed of a setting sun. I was frantically running west, trying desperately to catch it and remain in its fiery warmth and light. But I was losing the race. The sun was beating me to the horizon and was soon gone. I suddenly found myself in the twilight. Exhausted, I stopped running and glanced with foreboding over my shoulder to the east. I saw a vast darkness closing in on me. I was terrified by that darkness. I wanted to keep running after the sun, though I knew that it was futile, for it had already proven itself faster than I was. So I lost all hope, collapsed to the ground, and fell into despair. I thought in that moment that I would live in darkness forever. I felt absolute terror in my soul."[45]

Jerry embraced the darkness of his suffering and eventually found light again.

"...the quickest way for anyone to reach the sun and the light of day is not to run west, chasing after the setting sun, but to head east, plunging into the darkness until one comes to the sunrise."[46]

Dr. Sittser waited patiently for the sun to rise again on the eastern horizon, and rise it did, eventually. The addict, by contrast,

---

[45] *A Grace Disguised,* Gerald Sittser, Zondervan, 1995, p. 41.
[46] Ibid, p. 42.

cannot cease his endless pursuit of πορνεία. He refuses to accept that the sun could possibly set without him. He feels shortchanged, a victim of unfair circumstances, an innocent casualty in the war of life. He believes himself to be forever entitled to the sun's warmth and light. It had no right to set. He got a raw deal. If the setting sun is reality, then, by God, the addict will re-create reality. He will make his very own imitation ball of fire… rebound relationships, one-night stands, strip clubs, or any other form of erotica he needs to stay in the artificial glow. The man caught in the web of sexual addiction cannot accept the finality of pain. Somehow he feels unique and beyond suffering's reach.

The objective is not to avoid emotional pain, but rather to learn from it. The question of the source of our suffering is largely irrelevant. Some pain we bring on ourselves. Some is random and we did nothing to deserve it. According to the psalmist, the darkness of some of our losses comes directly from God and, in the words of Paul Simon, we reluctantly prepare our welcome: "Hello darkness my old friend; I've come to talk with you again."[47] We are left with little to do but embrace personal darkness as our "closest friend":

"You [God] *bring darkness,…"*
"You have taken from me friend and neighbor –
darkness is my closest friend."
Psalm 104.20a; 88.18 NIV 2011

Who can we blame for our suffering? God, Satan, ourselves, others, coincidence, happenstance, fate, the nature of the broken world in which we live? Or, no one and nothing at all? Soothing answers and logical explanations evaporate before us. We are left with nothing but a choice; the choice to embrace the darkness or pretend it's not there.

No person escapes the reality of emotional pain. Its eventuality marches toward us like an unrelenting army of irresistible force. The reality of loss and grief advances mercilessly and envelops every living soul in the power of its devastation and ruin.

According to Dr. Sittser, "Loss is a universal experience. Like

---

[47] Simon and Garfunkel's famous hit, *"The Sound of Silence,"* found its way to No. 1 on the Billboard Hot 100 record chart by January, 1966.

physical pain, we know it is real because sooner or later all of us experience it. But loss is also a solitary experience. Again, like physical pain, we know it is real only because we experience it uniquely within ourselves."[48] We therefore cannot easily quantify our suffering nor compare it with another's.

Early in his recovery process, an addict may express, "You don't know how I feel or understand what I've been through" as if to convince himself that he is unique. He wants to believe that his pain is so profound that he may rightfully justify his addiction. He's partially correct, of course. You can't know what he's suffered or how he feels, but neither does he know what you have suffered and how you feel. The simple truth remains: if you can get better, so can he. Hold on to this truth for yourself and every addict you know. The addict hopes to convince himself, and anyone else within earshot, that his pursuit of πορνεία is reasonable given the hard-life hand he was dealt. Although it is entirely appropriate to show him compassion and to empathize, even sympathize, with his situation, it is certainly not true that addiction is his only option. In this he is not correct.

We cannot outrun the lengthening shadows of sorrow, hurt, distress, or grief. We will never catch the setting sun. We must stop running west on the path of Judas and plunge, instead, into the darkness. Following in the footsteps of Peter, we choose to feel deeply our suffering, allowing it to shape the persons we are meant to become.

Relief to emotional pain is not always forthcoming. We may faithfully follow Jesus on the path of self-discovery and actively participate in personal recovery... and still feel the hurt. In these hard times, "Why?" takes on a special significance. It's not "Why me?" or "Why *must* I suffer?" but rather, "Why *do* I suffer?" There are reasons for the anguish in our souls, and some of those reasons become knowable only when we choose to absorb our pain and embrace the darkness.

> *"Though I sit in darkness,*
> *the LORD will be my light."*
> Micah 7.8c NIV

---

[48] Ibid, p. 171.

I am a big fan of the way Robert Plant croons out a tune. His rendition of "Darkness, Darkness" feels like a modern day psalm to me. It's raw and honest; acknowledging the reality of pain and the universal need for a light under the "blanket" of "endless night."

"Darkness, Darkness, be my pillow,
Take my head and let me sleep;
In the coolness of your shadow,
In the silence of your deep.

"Darkness, darkness, hide my yearning,
For the things I cannot see.
Keep my mind from constant turning,
To the things I cannot be.

"Darkness, darkness, be my blanket,
Cover me with the endless night.
Take away the pain of knowing,
Fill this emptiness with light; emptiness with light now.

"Darkness, darkness, long and lonesome,
Is the day that brings me here.
I have felt the edge of sadness,
I have known the depths of fear. "[49]

Imagine yourself on a bright, warm, sunny day gazing at a beautiful, blue sky. Do you know what you are you looking at? Stars! You're looking directly at stars, but you cannot see them. A magnificent collection of twinkling constellations lay hidden in the light. Your eyes cannot perceive them.

Like shining stars on a clear, black night, some of God's most brilliant epiphanies are viewable only in the darkness. Many truths can only be found in dark and difficult times, and there, the greatest of all truths, the knowledge of God Himself, awaits your apprehending.

---

[49] Robert Plant's version of "Darkness, Darkness" is found on his 2002 album *Dreamland.* It was originally written by Jesse Colin Young for his band The Youngbloods, and released on their 1969 album *Elephant Mountain.*

"The LORD reigns...
clouds and thick darkness surround Him."
Psalm 97.1-2 NAS

"I will give you treasures hidden in the darkness– secret riches.
I will do this so you may know that I am the LORD"
Isaiah 45.3 NLT

If it doesn't hurt, it isn't loss. All loss hurts... the loss of friends and loved ones, the loss of idealism and innocence, the loss of right standing with God and people. All loss hurts and all loss provides an opportunity to sit with pain; that is, to feel it without the numbing and temporal benefit of your addiction. When you say "no" to the pursuit of πορνεία, and choose to suffer instead, you are choosing the path of Peter whose words have encouraged believers for two millennia.

"Dear friends, do not be surprised at the painful trial you are *suffering, as though something strange were happening to you.* *But rejoice that you participate in the sufferings of Christ, so* *that you may be overjoyed when his glory is revealed."* 1st Peter 4:12-14 NIV 1984

Life is good, but never perfect. Disappointment, conflicts, betrayal, grief, and trauma are inevitable. Emotional pain is a part of the human condition – every human's condition. Prepare to suffer, but suffer with hope. Suffer redemptively. Embark on the journey of self-discovery. Trust Jesus and your brothers in recovery. Listen to the voice of your conscience. Flee πορνεία. Embrace the darkness. Wait patiently, and have hope.

"For God, who said, 'Let there be light in the darkness,' has *made this light shine in our hearts so we could know the glory* *of God that is seen in the face of Jesus Christ."* 2nd Corinthians 4.6 NLT

The sun will rise again; and "as surely as the sun rises, Yahweh will appear" (Hosea 6.3 WEB).

10 A NEW PASSION

The Beauty of a Woman

Behold the beauty of God's astonishing handiwork! Beauty surrounds us. Beautiful sunsets, beautiful art, beautiful trees, beautiful smiles, beautiful colors and sounds, beautiful minds and hearts, inner beauty, outer beauty, beautiful people, beautiful animals, beautiful stars, beautiful skies. It's a beautiful planet, a beautiful world, a beautiful universe. God designed it that way, and He "saw that it was good" (Genesis 1.25 NIV). Beauty surrounds us and, you may have noticed, beautiful women are everywhere. How could you possibly *not* notice? God made these gorgeous humans. We must learn to see a beautiful woman for exactly who she is; a remarkable creation by the God of all things beautiful.

"But how?" you ask. "The line between looking and lusting, seeing and craving, observing and objectifying, noticing and coveting is too narrow." Jesus offered a clue to the resolution of this dilemma in a prayer on behalf of His followers, including those of us who fight sexual temptation:

> *"I am not asking you to take them out of the world, but I ask you to protect them from the evil one. They do not belong to the world, just as I do not belong to the world."* John 17.15-16 NRSV

According to Jesus, we are *in* the world, but not *of* the world.

This distinction is significant in the realm of sexual addiction recovery. We "do not belong to the world," but neither do we belong to eternity, at least not yet. On the day of our death, we will be taken "out of the world." Until then, we must learn to navigate the subtle dissimilarity between a wholesome acknowledgment of divinely created beauty and an ungodly and lustful desire to possess it as our own.

This balanced approach requires both honesty and maturity:

1. We must stop lying to ourselves and endeavor to walk near the centerline on the path of purity. Our tendency toward waywardness brings us to the trail's edge, where we overestimate our ability to steer close to the 'slippery slope.' We try to believe that we may hover at the perimeter of πορνεία's vast wilderness, without falling into her dangerous ravines. What we really want, if we are honest, is a small dose of our sin; to catch a glimpse of, and thereby partially experience, what we know we cannot have.

2. Remaining on the proper path also requires maturity. We must finally "grow up in all aspects into Him who is the head, even Christ" (Ephesians 5.16 NASU). The recovering addict has to 'man up' and "grow up." He must occasionally "be crucified with Christ" (Galatians 2.20 KJV) and refuse to "gratify the desires of the flesh" (Galatians 5.16 RSV). It hurts to say "no" to πορνεία, but that's what mature men of God do.

Look straight ahead; don't even turn your head to look. Watch your step. Stick to the path and be safe. Don't sidetrack; pull back your foot from danger." Proverbs 4.25-27 TLB

God made stunning women. That's an unavoidable fact. You cannot make them disappear behind a shroud of baggy clothing, nor can you cover your head with a sack. You are "in the world" and you coinhabit this planet with beautiful females. They will occasionally cross your line of vision. Get used to it. A man "who looks at a woman" has not sinned. It is only the man "who looks at a woman *lustfully*" who has violated the command of Jesus in His famous 'Sermon on the Mount' (Matthew 5.28). This is the goal of sexual sobriety: *Learn to look without lust.* You cannot wear a blindfold everywhere you go nor can you make burkas standard issue for every attractive woman. But you can resist the temptation to mentally undress these amazing sisters, daughters, and mothers. No one is forcing you to objectify or sexualize them.

You are not unique and you are not alone. The enticement of illicit sexual pleasure runs as a common theme through all humanity in every generation. God is not singling you out or trying to trip you up. He is not teasing, taunting, or tempting you with His gift of womanhood. He expects you to depend on His grace to "grow up" and learn to love women as Jesus did. Yes, a few females may purposely flaunt their God-given attributes. Look away from the sexual gestures of these misguided ladies in media or in person. Learn to appreciate the inner and outer beauty of every human you encounter, including every woman. This approach to women is not only possible, it is commanded by Scripture:

"Treat older women as you would your mother, and treat younger women with all purity as you would your own sisters." 1st Timothy 5.2 NLT

Here's a self-evaluation comparison guide I developed for myself a few years ago. Perhaps you will find it helpful:

Sexualization Chart: "Choose wisely, and don't lie to yourself."	
Be human	Be an idolater
Be "in the world"	Be "of the world"
Notice her	Sexualize her
Look at her as a friend	Lust for her as a sex object
Appreciate her beauty	Mentally undress her
Acknowledge her beauty	Desire her for your own
Recognize her allure	Fantasize about her
Credit God for her beauty	Obsess on her beauty
See her as a sister	Deify her

About three years ago, I drove to a basketball game at Westview High School. My son, Robert, was representing the Beaverton Beavers as a JV player. As I entered the upper viewing level, my eye innocently caught the backside of a beautiful woman peering over the railing at the varsity contest. She was super attractive. I instantly acknowledged her beauty, smiled at this gift of God's creation, and then respectfully looked away. I did not sexualize her in my mind, but I certainly did notice her. The woman was positioned in a place and pose that made it impossible *not* to notice her. She was neither immodest nor overtly sexual, but she was absolutely stunning. This lady suddenly turned, smiled, and approached me. It was Adonica! I embraced my wife and quietly thanked God for the one woman on earth I could "have and hold as long as we both shall live."

If you are married, as I was, then "Be happy, yes, rejoice in the wife of your youth. Let her breasts and tender embrace satisfy you. Let her love alone fill you with delight" (Proverbs 5.18-19 TLB). Be extraordinarily grateful for the gifts of love, romance, and guilt-free sex with the woman you chose to cherish all the days of your remaining lives together. Treat all *other* women with utmost respect and dignity. When you notice an attractive woman, as you inevitably will, rejoice in God's incredible handiwork, and resist the temptation to 'check her out' sexually. Instead, press forward into the will of God, treating this beautifully created human being "with all purity" as you would "your mother" and "your own sisters."

Show Mercy… to Yourself and Others

You will occasionally fall below your sexual sobriety line. Show yourself the same mercy you would offer any other brother who suffered a lapse of judgment. Mercy is expensive and requires a little self-sacrifice. Judgment, even self-judgment, is cheap and easy to give. Like most things of value, mercy is rare. Judgment is everywhere. Merciful people set themselves apart from the crowd. Any fool can pass judgment. Cowards judge. Don't be a Judas to yourself and others on the journey of self-discovery. It takes courage to demonstrate mercy and forgive yourself on the days and in the moments you fail to walk in purity. When you stumble, make an immediate comeback, just like Peter did. Get back on the path, quickly. You're not perfect, but you're making progress on the journey of recovery. Don't give up.

"So speak and so act as those who are to be judged by the law of liberty. For judgment will be merciless to one who has shown no mercy; mercy triumphs over judgment." James 2.12-13 NASU

Kill the Porn Industry!

There is no greater threat to the emotional welfare of future generations than the Goliath of porn that has invaded our sacred land. Is there not a young David who will stand up against this mockery of everything that is pure and wholesome and cry out with conviction, "Who is this uncircumcised Philistine that he should defy the armies of the living God?" (1st Samuel 17.26 NIV). Make no mistake, πορνεία is a monstrous bully of GIGANTIC proportions. Did you know that, according to a 2013 poll, more people visit porn sites each month than the combined total of visitors to Netflix, Amazon, and Twitter?[50]

In the face of blatant sexual misconduct, Jesus turned the tables on a sinful woman's accusers: "The one of you who is without sin, let him be the first to throw a stone at her" (John 8.7 CJB). Jesus' act of mercy reminds us to focus on the real enemy. We must discover who the enemy *is* and who the enemy *isn't*. The enemy isn't the "woman caught in adultery." It isn't the boy who found and leered with sexual fascination at a *Hustler* magazine. It isn't the editor or publisher of *Hustler* magazine. It isn't the man who is hooked on endless hours of internet porn. It isn't that man's hurt and angry wife. It isn't the pimp, photographer, or perpetrator of pornography. It isn't the woman who strips for money. It isn't the man who frequents a strip club, and it isn't the one who judges those

---

[50] In the US Edition of a May 4th, 2013, Huffington Post article entitled "Porn Sites Get More Visitors Each Month than Netflix, Amazon and Twitter Combined," the writer quotes a 2013 infographic showing "estimated unique monthly visitors in millions" as Netflix.com (46M), Amazon.com (110M), Twitter.com (160M), and all porn sites (450M). http://www.huffingtonpost.com/2013/05/03/internet-porn-stats_n_3187682.html

who do.

The enemy is a spirit, a demon bearing the name 'πορνεία.' We must pick up stones and cast them, but not in the direction intended by "the teachers of the law and the Pharisees" who brought to Jesus the "woman caught in adultery" (John 8.3 NIV). Rather, each of us must rise up with fierce indignation and total abandon to drive our stones through the forehead of the detestable giant πορνεία, then cut off its ugly head. If David can kill Goliath, you and I can kill porn and the industry supporting it, no matter how colossal the task or improbable our success may seem. All we need is a little faith, and a bit of hope. Just as Jesus promised,

> *"For truly, I say to you, if you have faith like a grain of mustard seed, you will say to this mountain, 'Move from here to there,' and it will move, and nothing will be impossible for you."* Matthew 17.20 ESV

If we can move mountains, we can kill πορνεία. Together we can accomplish the impossible, even if it takes a lifetime, or longer. Theologian Reinhold Niebuhr claimed, "Nothing that is worth doing can be achieved in our lifetime; therefore we must be saved by hope."[51] Every attempt we make in the direction of cleansing our planet from the stain of πορνεία will make an eternal difference in many lifetimes to come. Have a little faith. There is hope.

I do not suggest a militant or political approach of directing our ire outward. "How *Not* to Kill the Porn Industry" might include such overused and largely ineffective tactics as sending letters to our legislators or picketing local adult bookstores or writing dogmatic articles in the local newspaper. These actions will be interpreted by many as the 'holier-than-thou' antics of frenzied, religious moralists. Such efforts may make participants feel better, but they will not help the cause. You will be dismissed as a fanatic on society's fringe. If you are serious about ending the porn epidemic, you must look at the guy in the mirror, and start with honest prayer

---

[51] *The Irony of American History,* Reinhold Niebuhr, Charles Scribner's Sons, 1952.

and real self-investigation.

Let's break down our noble objective into three steps. In Step 1, the individual becomes determined to eliminate πορνεία from his own life. He willingly engages in a recovery program like 423 Men with dependable brothers. As noted in Chapter 1 and the Afterword, the recovery process generally takes three to five years of hard work before essential sobriety is achieved. Purity is not cheap. Most of us spent many years following πορνεία into a deep, dark hole of hopelessness, so we should not be surprised when it takes us more time than expected to climb back out into freedom's light.

Once in the light, the commencement of Step 2 is marked by a holy ambition akin to the twelfth step in Alcoholics Anonymous:

> "Having had a spiritual awakening as the result of these steps, we tried to carry this message to alcoholics, and to practice these principles in all our affairs."

Many men who find help in 423 Men are empowered with a sense of hope and filled with a newfound passion to assist other guys in the battle to crush πορνεία.

I was never good at basketball, but I still remember a critical concept from fifth grade hoops. I could not shoot or dribble with any degree of proficiency, but I could steal. Coach asserted, however, "I'm glad you can force the turnover, Scriven, but it is not a valid possession until you have enough control to pass the ball to a teammate." Similarly, my success in recovery is not proven until I am able to adeptly pass the ball of purity to another brother on the court of sexual sobriety. The best leaders in 423 Men are broken men who, having experienced success in their own recovery, become passionate to help other struggling brothers on their journey of self-discovery.

In summary:

Step 1: Get healed sexually (e.g., stop πορνεία in your life).

Step 2: Help others heal sexually (e.g., stop πορνεία in others).

Now, for the third and final step:

Step 3: Kill the porn industry (e.g., stop πορνεία in society).

In tackling a task as monumental as ending porn, we start with the premise that every one of us who ever previewed illicit and sexually suggestive material becomes responsible for its existence. Each time a man clicks on a pornographic site, he is endorsing it. The porn industry is perpetuated by the demand for it. It's a case of supply and demand economics. In his brilliant TEDx talk, Ran Gavrieli stated, "I stopped watching porn because... I came to realize [that] by watching porn I take part in creating a demand for filmed prostitution, because that's what porn really is – filmed prostitution... Prostitution was nobody's childhood dream. It is always the result of trouble and distress."[52]

Little girls do not dream of becoming porn stars, strippers, or prostitutes. These precious children fell into it and, through a set of unfortunate circumstances, were forced, pimped, or cornered (or so they thought) into a career path in the sex trades. I raised four girls. Not one of them ever told me, "Daddy, when I grow up, I want to use my body to sexually entice men. I hear there's good money in that." No! Each one of their childhood dreams resembled the others – "I want to be a princess," or "I want to have horsies and take care of animals," or "I want to be a mommy just like Mommy." Why do 'good girls,' little princesses-in-the-making, become so-called 'bad girls'? Because someone lied to them, offering attention, love, cash, freedom, stardom, or hope for a life worth living, and these precious daughters and sisters bought the lie. Someone took advantage of their innocence for personal sexual gratification or the lure of easy money.

The women of pornography, the objects of our lust, have job security because we too bought a lie: "Pornography doesn't hurt anyone." The porn industry didn't create that lie. We did. You and I invented this untruth. We chose to believe that porn use was somehow more acceptable than other forms of πορνεία because we weren't hurting anyone by watching it. Why did we tell this 'lie to self'? Because we wanted to watch young, beautiful, naked women

---

[52] "Why I stopped watching porn" is a TEDx Talk by Ran Gavrieli published October 26th, 2013, earning well over thirteen million views. You can easily Google search and view on YouTube.

engaging in sexual activities. It's that simple. May we repent and forever reject the false claim that pornography is a victimless activity. Our use of porn amounts to nothing less than participation in "filmed prostitution," just as Mr. Gavrieli said. Somebody gets paid to pose. We pay to watch. We pay with our lives: our time, energy, creativity, imagination, integrity, and sometimes even our money.

The hard truth is simple:
Porn exists because we want it. If we didn't, it wouldn't.

The solution to the problem of pornography is also simple:
Stop using it.

This solution is not as unattainable as it may first appear. As discussed in Chapter 1, recovery in 423 Men looks like "progress, not perfection." Consider, for example, the man who replaces his practice of viewing graphic online pornography with a new bad habit. He chooses instead to arouse himself with erotic fantasies of his own making. While his choice is certainly not a picture of "perfection," it is also not the endpoint in his journey of recovery. The transition from active use of pornography to mental, sexual visualization can represent a small step of "progress" in the man's personal recovery. It is similar to the strategy behind the nicotine patch for the smoker who wants to quit, or methadone for a heroin addict.

This 'maintenance therapy' is not the goal of recovery, but I would rather a man entertain wrong sexual thoughts than to both view porn *and* entertain wrong sexual thoughts, as every single internet porn user does. I am not condoning any act of sexual misbehavior, whether conceptual or perceptual. Rather, I am actively denouncing the use of printed or filmed, soft or hard-core pornography, and applauding every man who makes an ironclad agreement within himself to stop its use, no matter where else he may be on the recovery continuum. His decision to transition from visual to mental fantasies can represent a single, albeit small, stride in the direction of sexual sobriety. Without the stimulation of graphic pornography, the addict's illicit stimulation and sexual novelty factor will decrease, and his resolution is accompanied by an added bonus: one less man clicking on porn sites.

A man ending his dependence on pornographic images and film is another step toward the objective of drying up the demand for published πορνεία. We can kill the porn industry by choking it at the source. If you and I choose to quit viewing pornography, we lower the demand, and make incremental, yet vital tactical progress toward damming the flood of πορνεία, with the help of one surviving porn user at a time.

"Tens of thousands of people have tried abstaining from sexually stimulating material in a process they call 'rebooting,'" so states a Goodreads reviewer of *Your Brain on Porn* by Gary Wilson.[53] Why not join the anti-porn movement and allow yourself to be 'conquered by a new passion'? Why not enlist others in the war on pornography? Why not cast your vote against an immoral and destructive industry by refusing to participate in it? Together we can put an end to this blight of epidemic proportions. It can be done. Have hope and a little "faith." Do not "shrink back" from the challenge:

> " '...*my righteous one will live by faith.*
> *My soul takes no pleasure in anyone who shrinks back.* '
>
> *But we are not among those who shrink back and so are lost,*
> *but among those who have faith and so are saved.*"
> Hebrews 10.38-39 NRSV, quoting Habakkuk 2.4[54]

Rise up, O man of God, with the indignation of Phinehas.[55] Thrust your spear through the lure of secret sin in your own heart. Do your part to end the plague of πορνεία in the land your children will inherit. Make a firm decision this day, not to view pornography. "Don't worry about tomorrow," as Jesus said, for "Tomorrow will

---

[53] *Your Brain on Porn – Internet Pornography and the Emerging Science of Addiction*, Gary Wilson, Foreword by Dr. Jack Anthony, Commonwealth Publishing, 2014. Also, check out Mr. Wilson's groundbreaking TEDx talk at https://www.youtube.com/watch?v=wSF82AwSDiU, which has garnered over seven million views.

[54] The writer of Hebrews is not quoting the Hebrew Scriptures, but rather the Septuagint (LXX), the Greek translation of Habakkuk 2.4.

[55] See Numbers 25.1-8.

worry about itself" (Matthew 6.34 HCSB). Stop making promises you cannot keep. "I will never, never, never do that again," does not work. Trust Jesus and just say "No!" to porn today. Then, squarely face anyone who will listen, and declare with the audacity of Paul, "Imitate me."[56] We can kill the porn industry, starting right now with you and me. "No porn today!"

Let a New Passion Conquer You

I was standing in church somewhere around the turn of the millennium. We were preparing for communion at Sunset Presbyterian Church. I was active in my recovery group and enjoying a new level of sexual sobriety for the first time in thirty-five years. My beautiful wife, Adonica, was standing by my side as we held the bread and cup in our hands, ready to partake. In that holy moment, I noticed two young ladies in front of me. They were wearing tight jeans and had nice figures. Don't ask me how I knew that. I did not look at these Christian sisters in a sexual way. But somehow I knew. Like many men, I have been cursed with sexual radar and can quickly locate all gorgeous ladies in any large crowd. Attractive women, tight jeans, low lights, soft worship music. I don't mean to sound sacrilegious, but the setting was positively seductive. Would there be any harm in a quick glance? It was a familiar question. I considered doing what I had always done: to sexualize these young women in my mind. Then, I heard the voice of Jesus.

"You can look if you want, or you can have a ministry with men. But you can't have both, and the choice is yours."

I knew precisely what He meant. I had a decision to make at the crossroads of sobriety. No one could make it for me, not even Jesus. No one, besides Jesus, would ever know if I made the wrong decision. It was my choice, and mine alone.

Nearly 1,500 years before the first coming of Christ, Moses

---

[56] See 1st Corinthians 4.16 NIV and other verses related to imitating, modeling, and following the example of those who follow Jesus: 1st Corinthians 11.1; Philippians 3.17; 1st Thessalonians 1.6; 2nd Thessalonians 3.7, 9. Be the man others emulate with a life devoted to killing πορνεία one day at a time.

presented a similar choice to the people of Israel.

"This day I call heaven and earth as witnesses against you that I have set before you life and death, blessings and curses. <u>Now choose life</u>, so that you and your children may live and that you may love the LORD your God, listen to his voice, and hold fast to him. For the LORD is your life..." Deuteronomy 30.19-20 NIV 1984

At this critical point, early in my recovery, I chose life. No one could have made that decision for me, but I could not have made the right decision alone. I needed help from God and my brothers in recovery. I did not look down to 'check out' the beautiful sisters in Christ who stood just inches away. Instead, I kept my gaze forward.

"Let your eyes look directly forward, and your gaze be straight before you." Proverbs 4.25 ESV

I made the right choice that day. It wasn't easy; in fact, it was downright painful. I wanted my sex hit and self-denial felt awful. Yet, inside I wore the smile of godly satisfaction. I knew angels leapt for joy over my victory in that moment. I passed a small test and proved to myself that I wanted effective ministry more than πορνεία. It felt good. I was energized in a new way. I partook of the Eucharist on that eventful day with a clear conscience.

My pastor, Dominic Done, encouraged our congregation in a recent Sunday sermon. "The best way to conquer an old passion is to be conquered by a new one."[57] My new passion began eighteen years ago on Communion Sunday at Sunset Presbyterian. There and then, I chose to conquer an old passion with a new one. Today, I am still motivated to serve men caught in the web of sexual addiction. Call me "Driven Scriven." I am unashamedly and passionately devoted to assisting men in the pursuit of healthy sexuality. If I can find freedom from sexual bondage, then anybody can. If Jesus can use a fallen and broken guy like me, then He can use anyone for His redemptive purposes.

---

[57] *"Self-Control"*, sermon series on "Fruit of the Spirit", Dominique Done, Westside A Jesus Church, June 5th, 2016.

"If anyone is thirsty, let him come to Me and drink. He who believes in Me, as the Scripture said, 'From his innermost being will flow rivers of living water.'" John 7.37-38 NASU

The springs of living water about which Jesus spoke cannot flow freely through a man who is consumed with lust and driven by uncontrolled fantasies of forbidden pleasure. Proverbs 4.23 commands every human, "Guard your heart with all diligence, for from it flow the springs of life." There is a reason to guard your heart. The reason is the promise of life.

In Robert Louis Stevenson's classic novel of the battle for dominance between opposing inner forces, Dr. Lanyon recounts the horror of virtuous Dr. Jekyll's resolve to rid himself once and for all of the malicious Mr. Hyde.

> "He put the glass to his lips and drank at one gulp. A cry followed; he reeled, staggered, clutched at the table and held on, staring with injected eyes, gasping with open mouth; and as I looked there came, I thought, a change – he seemed to swell – his face became suddenly black and the features seemed to melt and alter – and the next moment, I had sprung to my feet and leaped back against the wall, my arm raised to shield me from that prodigy, my mind submerged in terror.

> "'O God!' I screamed, and 'O God!' again and again; for there before my eyes – pale and shaken, and half fainting, and groping before him with his hands, like a man restored from death – there stood Henry Jekyll!"[58]

My "mind was submerged in [the] terror" of sexual addiction. I too "screamed 'O God!' again and again" throughout my many years of bondage. I emerged from the painful ordeal "like a man restored from death." I am a new man, the man I was destined to be before I drank from πορνεία's dirty cup. I "put the glass to [my] lips and drank at one gulp" of the water Jesus and my brothers in recovery offered. I was given a second chance at life, a chance to

---

[58] *The Strange Case of Dr. Jekyll and Mr. Hyde*, Robert Louis Stevenson, first published 1886, A Signet Classic, 1978, pp. 101-102.

drink deeply of the pure, eternally thirst-busting water Jesus freely held out for me.

"Whoever drinks of this water will thirst again, but whoever drinks of the water that I shall give him will never thirst. But the water that I shall give him will become in him a fountain of water springing up into everlasting life." John 4.13-14 NKJV

I am a new man. I am conquered by a new passion. I am forever grateful to Jesus Christ and my brothers in recovery.

AFTERWORD

In this book, I endeavored to offer hope to those ensnared in the web of πορνεία. I also tried to demonstrate in the preceding chapters the importance of a sexual recovery ministry in the local church; that is, to provide the biblical foundation for a ministry like 423 Men and the philosophical reasons for its existence.

This Afterword offers practical application of small group fundamentals and leadership principles we promote in 423 Men. All documents used in the operation of our recovery program are included in the Appendices.

Curriculum and Meeting Management

A recovery group, even a church sponsored recovery program like 423 Men, is not a Bible study. We do not meet in group to learn about the travels of the Apostle Paul, investigate the symbolism of the Tabernacle, or parse Greek verbs. If a guy is looking for a systematic study of Scripture, we direct him elsewhere. Our program is not about the acquisition of Bible knowledge. The goal of recovery is not information, but transformation. It is entirely possible for a man to possess a nearly encyclopedic grasp of Scripture, and yet remain stuck in an addictive pattern of sexual misbehavior. In fact, some guys hide behind their knowledge of theology and Bible as an avoidance tactic to keep from addressing the real issue of secret sexual sin. Each incoming 423 member authorizes a document that includes the statement, "I realize that the Bible may be discussed more or less than I would like it to be."[59] In 423 Men we hold a high view of Scripture. We believe that "all Scripture is inspired by God and profitable for teaching, for reproof, for correction, for training in righteousness; that the man of God may be adequate, equipped for every good work" (2nd Timothy 3.16-17 NAS) and we employ God's written word to those ends.

The Bible, of course, has a fair amount to say on the subject of healthy sexuality. 423 Men curricula are heavily based on Scripture and sprinkled generously with references from the books of Genesis through Revelation. We also strongly encourage 423 members to engage in P. B. & J. No, that does not stand for peanut butter and jelly. In the context of Christ-centered recovery, we advise men to practice the devotional disciplines of prayer, Bible reading, and journaling (P. B. & J.). We remind members, "Take a few minutes during the best part of your day for dedicated prayer and Bible reading. Then record your insights in a journal." A journal is a private collection of biblically inspired thoughts about your journey of self-discovery as directed by the Holy Spirit. Sometimes the men "share their P. B. & J." by reading from their journals during group for mutual encouragement. Men in the program are not expected to spend inordinate amounts of time in this devotional practice. They are busy with jobs and family obligations. I would rather a guy consistently practice five minutes of P. B. & J. each day for years, than to invest lengthy hours in the study of the Word, prayer, and journal writing early in his recovery, only to soon suffer burnout. Hefty levels of energy dedicated to P. B. & J. may not be sustainable. Consistency is the key to a healthy practice of devotional disciplines. The twentieth century French philosopher Blaise Pascal is reported as saying, "All of humanity's problems stem from man's inability to sit quietly in a room alone."[60] Even a few daily moments

---

[59] From *"423 Agreement"* included in the Appendix of this book.
[60] Blaise Pascal (1623-1662) "Fragment *Entertainment* No. 4/7" (Laf. 136, salt. 168) transcripts of the C1 and C2 copies: "J'ay dit souvent que tout le malheur des hommes vient d'une seule chose qui est de ne sçavoir pas demeurer en repos dans une chambre," may be translated literally, "I have often said that all the misfortune[s] of men [come from] just one thing, that is not knowing how to stay quietly in a room." You may find and view fragments of Pascal's actual manuscripts at a variety of sites on the Internet.

spent alone with Jesus and away from the noise of technology and people, can help to center a man's soul and pave the way for the Holy Spirit's leading.

"For all who are led by the Spirit of God are children of God." Romans 8.14 NRSV

If the Bible is spiritual food, then a well-written, Bible-based book by a qualified author on the subject of healthy sexuality is brain food. 423 Men groups use various curricula to stimulate meaningful conversation and ensure that groups remain well-rounded on the subject matter. Books selected for use in 423 Men must be biblically sound and are typically written by men who have personal experience in overcoming the enticement of πορνεία. 423 Men is not a curriculum-driven program, so new guys can join any time there is a vacancy. They do not need to wait until the group starts a new book. While important, the curriculum is not the main feature of time spent in a group recovery setting. The majority of group time is given to open discussion and personal sharing. About forty-five minutes at nearly every meeting are devoted to a group dialogue on a short assigned lesson from one of the books approved for use in the program. Weekly homework typically requires about thirty minutes of reading by each member in preparation for group.

423 Men promotes the K.I.S.S. method of meeting management.[61] We start on time, open with prayer, go over the attendance roster, read the "423 Men Guidelines," discuss the curriculum, and conduct the "sharing of weeks."[62] During "weeks," each guy reminds the group of his sexual sobriety line and then reports on his successes as well as failures with sexual sin and lust issues during the previous seven days. Members may ask clarifying questions of the guy sharing his week, but leaders will not allow them to "cross-talk, offer advice, or preach at other members of the group."[63] Men are encouraged to answer for themselves the "Why?" question in an effort to get at the underlying reasons for addictive behavior patterns. Most guys talk for about five minutes during

---

[61] K.I.S.S. stands for "Keep it simple, stupid!"
[62] See "'Sharing Your Week' Guidelines" included in the Appendix of this book.
[63] Item 12 on *"Typical 423 Meeting"* included at the Appendix of this book.

"weeks." Timers are often used to restrict a tendency toward verbal rambling and to help guys remain focused on the purpose of their sharing. Groups generally offer a short break around the halfway point of the meeting. In closing, members often huddle up for prayer and always end on time. Meetings are two hours long. It's okay to finish early, but never late.

About once a month, a 423 Men group will highlight a particular member who is "given an opportunity to share his personal story of struggle with sexual sin."[64] This is a twenty to thirty minute detailed account of the man's sexual history with an emphasis on how Jesus is delivering him from the cycle of shame and the control of πορνεία. The practice is inspirational for everyone in the group and helps create a community bonding.

> *"Let the redeemed of the LORD tell their story—*
> *those he redeemed from the hand of the foe…"*
> Psalm 107.2 NIV 2011

For the majority of guys, knowing why they act out sexually is enough to get better and stay better. But they cannot do this alone. Addicts need addicts to show them the way. All men with sexually addictive behavior patterns need a recovery group to get better. Some may require counseling in addition to group. 423 Men is not therapy and 423 leaders are not therapists. They are qualified only by life experience, and not by professional training, to facilitate meetings. That's all. Leaders must quickly refer men to more qualified counselors when that becomes necessary. They are also instructed to notify 423 management immediately if a member sounds suicidal or reveals he is involved in or aware of any form of abuse.[65]

Getting sexually healthy does not happen overnight. If they work their recovery program, most men can graduate from 423 Men with excellent sexual sobriety in three to five years. The goal is to give these men tools to live in purity for the rest of their lives and, in so doing, equip them to serve effectively in their families, churches, and communities. Some graduates occasionally return for

---

[64] Item 10 on *"Typical 423 Meeting"* included at the Appendix of this book.
[65] See *"423 Agreement"* included in the Appendix of this book.

a little 'continuing education.' Ongoing support is available and men who return for additional help are always welcome. Some men remain in 423 Men as leaders, because they have a passion to help other guys trapped in the cycle of shame and sexual addiction.

Respect

If 423 Men is about nothing else, it is about respect. We respect each other in the program, and show it in practical ways: [66]

When a man is talking, we look him in the eye and pay attention. We don't interrupt, allow our minds to wander, or choose that moment to send a text.

When we leave or transfer from our 423 Men group, we do so respectfully by speaking first to our leaders and then saying goodbye in person to our group. Besides showing great respect to the members of our group, this practice helps to provide proper emotional closure.

We guard against offending each other and work out our differences privately, outside of group. We don't ignore the problem, nor do we behave passively aggressive toward any brother in group.

We hold our recovery brothers in high esteem and, no matter what they share in group, we choose to believe the best about them.

We refuse to intentionally violate the anonymity or confidentiality of any member of 423 Men.

We trust that each member has a direct connection with Jesus, and we will not act as a man's conscience. "All of us are free to find our own answers" in our journey of self-discovery.

---

[66] See items 1, 2, 4, 5, 8, and 10 on *"423 Small Group Guidelines"* included in the Appendix of this book.

We do not make excuses, but attend the meetings and complete assigned homework, just like every other man in the program.

When a man feels respected, he can start to breathe more easily. He swells with confidence to do the right thing. He gets a sudden burst of energy and recognizes he is in a place of hope. Every man is respect-worthy, if for no other reason, because he was made "in the image of God" (Genesis 1.27; 9.6 NIV) and bears "the likeness of God" (James 3.9 NAS). A man's *imago Dei* earns him the right of respect, no matter what he has done or failed to do. We do not pass judgment on anyone in the program. We were created equal, and each one of us has equally violated God's moral standards. None of us can claim to be any better, or worse, than any other guy sitting next to us in a meeting. We are all deserving of God's wrath, yet we are all recipients of His pardon. Jesus shed his blood for every single 423 man; therefore, we have no business judging anyone. Instead, we have every reason to respect every man we meet in 423 and, for that matter, every person we encounter in this world. When a man feels he is a respected member of the 423 community, he is imbued with new resolve to take the next step on his journey toward healing.

Attendance

Attendance at weekly meetings is crucial for recovery. We regularly remind the men in the program, "This is America, the land of the free. You don't have to be in 423 Men. The decision to join is yours. But, if you want to be in 423 Men, then you must be 'all in.'" 423 Men meetings are not optional. When a man joins, he makes a conscious choice to comply with the attendance guideline at his intake interview:

"We agree to be here every week, on time, unless there is an urgent and unavoidable scheduling conflict or genuine emergency. We will call the group leader to explain in advance when we cannot attend or must be late."[67]

---

[67] Item 4 on *"423 Small Group Guidelines"* included in the Appendix of this book.

While there are valid reasons for missing group (e.g., serious illness, out of town vacation or occasional business trip, car wreck, even an unexpected traffic jam), we do not allow guys to come and go at will. We expect members to declare themselves as either 'in or out' and, if they are 'in,' then they make a rock-solid commitment to weekly attendance. Nothing is gained by half-hearted, mediocre effort in the war we wage against sexual addiction. Jesus had hard words for 'fence-sitters,' 'middle-of-the-roaders,' and 'luke-warmers':

> *"I know your deeds, that you are neither cold nor hot. I wish you were either one or the other! So, because you are lukewarm — neither hot nor cold — I am about to spit you out of my mouth."* Revelation 3.15-16 NIV

A man's 423 group is a community of recovery and support. He cannot get better if he is not present and accounted for. Since "we are no longer to be children, tossed here and there by waves [of πορνεία] and... [Satan's] craftiness in deceitful scheming" (Ephesians 4.14 NASU), we must take our recovery seriously and make the wise, and sometimes difficult, choice to show up at meetings. The decision for active involvement in group will help to stabilize a man in his pursuit of sexual sobriety.

If a member falters in his attendance without notifying his group leaders with a valid reason, they will try to reach out to him. If the absent brother fails to respond, leaders will adapt as necessary and send an email similar to the one below. All group leaders and the 423 Men administrator are copied (not blind copied) into the email. This procedure has two benefits. First, it demonstrates to the missing brother that the program has integrity. We take the attendance guideline seriously and won't allow men to easily and quietly slip away without a formal acknowledgment. The absentee individual learns that we all care about him and his absenteeism has an impact on the group. It formalizes the truant brother's departure and reminds him that the door for his return is always open. Second, it has the logistical benefit of signaling the 423 administrator to fill the vacancy with another man on the waiting list.

Hi _____,

We miss seeing you in 423 Men. You have always been a vital part of the group and your absence is felt. As you know, our guidelines state, "We agree to be here every week, on time, unless there is an urgent and unavoidable scheduling conflict or genuine emergency. We will call the group leader to explain in advance when we cannot attend or must be late." _____, we have not heard from you, even though I have texted [or left voice messages, etc.]. I hope you are okay.

Shall we assume you are no longer interested in 423 Men? I hope that is not the case, but we have no way of knowing since you have not responded to my texts [or voice messages, etc.]. Please know we love and miss you.

I will inform the group of my attempts to reach you and will remove you from the roster. If it is your intention to remain in our group then, of course, we want you to stay, but you will need to make a renewed commitment to weekly attendance.

If you decide you would like to come back to our group or rejoin 423 Men anytime in the future, please contact [_the 423 administrator_]. He will place you on the waiting list and you can join any group with an opening matching your schedule.

Thanks, _____ .

Sincerely,

_____

The goal of this outreach campaign is to gently restore the brother who slips away if he is still stuck in the cycle of shame. It is intended as a loving and pastoral gesture in the spirit of Jesus' parable about a single lost sheep recorded in the gospel of Luke:

"Suppose one of you had a hundred sheep and lost one. Wouldn't you leave the ninety-nine in the wilderness and go

after the lost one until you found it? When found, you can be sure you would put it across your shoulders, rejoicing, and when you got home call in your friends and neighbors, saying, 'Celebrate with me! I've found my lost sheep!'" Luke 15:4-6 *The Message*

Shepherds pursue wayward sheep who are at high risk for relapse. This is what 423 leaders do on behalf of their 423 flocks. Paul challenged the early church, "Brethren, if a man is overtaken in any trespass, you who are spiritual restore such a one in a spirit of gentleness, considering yourself lest you also be tempted" (Galatians 6.1 NKJV).

Πορνεία is deadly. We are engaged in a battle of eternal life and death and 423 Men is always there to reach out and receive lost brothers into the fold. No man should quietly slink away from 423 Men. A good departure is a celebratory occasion because it means a member found and maintained the standard of sexual sobriety he was hoping to achieve when he joined 423 Men. The graduate feels strong, well connected to Jesus and his recovery brothers in the on-going victory over πορνεία. His 'goodbye' is accompanied by cheers of triumph, attaboy's, and a reminder that he may return anytime he feels the need to strengthen his resolve to live in purity. Some successful brothers remain in 423 Men as leaders both because they want to maintain their sexual sobriety and because they have a passion to assist their brothers in the battle.

The Danger of Well-Intended Advice

We should distinguish between help and advice. Most advice, is unhelpful, especially that which is offered in the moment, without careful thought and prayer. Why should we think we know what's best for another? As previously stated, advice-giving can be a subtle way of introducing shame and judgment, especially in a group setting. Real help is most often imparted by the gift of active listening and honest self-disclosure. If I am transparent with my sexual struggles, then I give permission for my brother to do the same. If I truly listen to him, look him in the eye, show empathy, nod in agreement, ask clarifying questions, and, of course, stop looking at my phone when he is talking, then he learns to trust me. Trust is fundamental in the act of full disclosure. At 423 Men, we are all on a level playing field. No member is any better or worse than another. We are on this journey of self-discovery together. By eliminating advice in a recovery meeting, we build trust and show respect to our brother's own unique discovery process. We make room for the Holy Spirit to teach and impart truth.

It is legitimate to ask questions for clarification after a man confesses his sin in a meeting, as long it is not a backdoor form of advice-giving. If, for example, a guy discloses, "I masturbated in the shower every day this week" and another member of the group inquires, "Have you tried cold showers?," his question is neither honest nor innocent. It is advice. He simply advised, "Try cold showers," while posing it as a question.

There are two main dangers in advice-giving at a recovery meeting.

1. It could make the man receiving advice feel inferior to the one offering advice. It is a form of condescension. If counseling of this kind is allowed in recovery meetings, the net effect will be more silence and less disclosure by the man receiving advice, as well as others observing the interaction.

2. It could replace the work of the Holy Spirit in the man receiving advice. Recovery is about helping participants find answers within themselves. Even when addicts want advice, they must learn instead to hear and depend directly on the voice of Jesus for the help they seek.

Not all advice is harmful. We cannot preclude the possibility of good advice or even an authentic prophetic word offered by the prompting of the Spirit. But "the spirits of the prophets are subject to the prophets" (1st Corinthians 14.32 KJV). That's a nice way of saying, 'Anyone, even a prophet, can keep his mouth shut.' Paul made this point so church meetings could be conducted "properly and in an orderly manner" (1st Corinthians 14.40 NAS). 423 Men meetings also run "properly and in an orderly manner." Check out the version of this text found in the Amplified Bible:

"For the spirits of the prophets (the speakers in tongues) are under the speaker's control [and subject to being silenced as may be necessary]."

I often remind members of 423 Men that there are 168 hours in a week. "Give all the advice you want. Just do it outside of group. You have a full 166 hours each week to offer counsel, if you must." Advice, cross-talk, or preaching are unwelcome during 423 Men group meeting times.

Advice is often cheap. It's easy to give in the moment and costs the advice-giver nearly nothing. Advice worth giving should be thoughtful and prayerful. When a man feels compelled to give a word of direction to another brother in his group, he should first submit it privately to the Lord for approval after the meeting. Taking time to pray and consider his words before voicing them increases the likelihood of their meaningful impact and a positive outcome. If the man giving the word will invite the object of his message out for coffee, then he has probably earned the right to give advice. If his advice is not worth a cup of Starbucks and an hour of his time, then it is not worth sharing. If advice costs us nothing to offer, it is probably worth exactly that... *nothing*. Cheap advice is the worst form of condescension, and we must avoid it at all costs.

Leadership

We do not import leaders. 423 Men leaders are home grown, having come to the program for the same reasons and through the same channels as every other man. A leader possesses basic leadership skills recognizable by the members of his group and, by virtue of his hard work in personal recovery, is himself experiencing progressive sexual sobriety. 423 Men leaders are qualified to lead, but are not expected to be perfect. Rather, leaders are men with the integrity to be real, transparent, and authentic on their path of recovery. Most leaders do not feel qualified when first approached to serve in this capacity, an attitude which, ironically, reinforces their readiness. New leaders are recommended by current leaders, and we address the following policies with all incoming leaders before they step into an active leadership role:

1. Leaders in 423 Men are not preachers. 423 leadership is not a "pulpit" opportunity. It is not a soapbox to promote pet doctrines, political views, or wealth of knowledge on any subject. Leaders help group members stay on the subject and avoid "debates about controversial topics and outside issues unrelated to healthy sexuality."[68]

2. There are two levels of leadership in 423 Men: co-leaders and support leaders. Two co-leaders share responsibility for the success of meetings. They typically take turns leading from week to week to give each other breaks and avoid leader burnout. Support leaders fill understudy roles, preparing to take the helm as a new co-leader when a current co-leader transfers to another group, drops from the program, moves away, or must step aside for any reason.

3. All leaders, both co-leaders and support leaders, are required to attend 423 Men leadership development meetings which are scheduled monthly.

4. Prospective leaders are asked to read and fully subscribe to the "423 Men Leader Qualifications and Responsibilities" document which is included in the Appendix of this book.

5. A 423 Men leader is aware of his high calling and responsibility and, consequently, does not step away from leadership without leaving his group in better condition than he found it. In that spirit, a departing leader makes a genuine effort to find and recommend his replacement.

6. All 423 leaders must complete a background check to be reviewed by the 423 Board as required by 423 Communities International's insurance carrier.

---

[68] Item 9 on *"423 Small Group Guidelines"* included in the Appendix of this book.

7. 423 Men leaders occasionally and willingly give up a degree of anonymity when church leaders, like pastors or elders, request a list of 423 leaders serving their church members.

423 Men leadership is facilitative rather than didactic in its approach to group management. Leaders model the 'do not preach at or lecture' guideline. 423 Men leaders are judged by how well they get everyone in group talking approximately equally. Some members are naturally verbose and have a hard time shutting up or staying on topic, and when given a chance to share, they over-share. Other men are shy and will sit through a meeting without uttering a peep, if allowed. A good leader will gently shut down the over-talker and warmly draw out the shy guy. This can be delicate, but is necessary for the well-being of any group. A dominating personality with too much to say can kill a meeting, and 423 leaders are trained not to allow that to happen.

Wise leaders apply this group dynamic principle: *Group members emotionally invest in the group success when they verbally contribute to the group process.* Quiet men who are not drawn out or expected to talk will soon drop out of the program. Over-talkers who say more than they should, ironically, also tend to leave group. Both are looking for guidance, which 423 leaders must provide.

Group leaders do not teach in words, but by example. They facilitate discussion. A skillful leader carefully reads the homework assignment and develops thoughtful, probing, open-ended questions to aid in group discussion. Given the limitations of time, it may occasionally happen that a 423 leader will talk less than a typical member.

While 423 leadership is an unglamorous, servant-style role, it is, nevertheless, enormously rewarding. It is an incredible privilege to assist men in prying themselves from πορνεία's insidious and firmly attached grasp. It is a personal calling and a form of mentoring at the highest and deepest levels. Leadership in 423 is a personification of Jesus' Great Commission to "go and make disciples" recorded in Matthew 28.18-20. 423 Men leadership is not for the faint of heart. Wimps need not apply. It's a dirty ministry, without accolades, and not naturally spoken of in polite conversation. Yet, it is a rich and fulfilling pastoral care opportunity for those so called. Leaders are instrumental in changing the lives of men, their families, churches, communities, and the world.

423 leaders follow Jude's mandate to the early church. They "save" guys by "snatching them out of the fire" of God's holy judgment and πορνεία's grip of death.

"And have mercy on those who doubt; save others by snatching them out of the fire..." Jude 23 ESV

Without passionate, Jesus-called leaders, 423 Men would cease to exist.

APPENDICES

The following pages contain all documents used in the 423 Men program and may be used by other churches or organizations wishing to implement a sexual recovery program. Two of these forms were adapted from Pure Desire Ministries with permission by Dr. Ted Roberts and Pure Desire Ministries, with credit at the bottom of each form.

For help in starting 423 Men at your church, please contact 423 Men at:

Email: info@423communities.org

Website: www.423communities.org

Confidential: (503) 898-0423

Mail: PO Box 1055
                Beaverton, OR 97075

Thank you.

List of Bible Version Abbreviations

423 Application

A 423 Communities leader has discussed the following forms with me:

- ☐ 423 Application
- ☐ 423 Agreement
- ☐ Typical 423 Meeting
- ☐ 423 Small Group Guidelines
- ☐ 423 Cycle of Shame

Name _____

Address _____

City State Zip _____

Phone(s) _____

Email(s) _____

Marital Status _____ Age _____

Home Church _____

I have been given the opportunity to ask questions about each of the above forms and agree to their conditions. I am at least 18 years old and I want to join a 423 Men group. If I am 18 years old or younger and wish to join 423 Young Men, my parent or guardian has authorized both this application below and the attached 423 Agreement.

- ☐ I agree to receive regular information by email from 423 Men.

X _____   _____
Applicant Signature   Date

X _____   _____
Parent/Guardian Signature (if applicant is under 18 years old)   Date

Application fee of $20 includes a copy of *The Pursuit of Porneia* by Dave Scriven. There is no additional cost for the 423 recovery program, except the purchase of book(s) used in your group.

423 Agreement

I understand that every attempt will be made to guard my anonymity and confidentiality in this group, but that it cannot be absolutely guaranteed in a group setting.

I realize that the group leader cannot control the actions of others in the group. I realize that confidentiality is sometimes broken accidentally and without malice.

I understand that I may share my own personal experiences in group with others outside group. I also understand that disclosing the identity or any information about others in the group with those outside group is strictly prohibited and may result in termination from 423.

I understand that the group leader is morally and ethically obligated to discuss with me if he observes any of the following behaviors which may lead to the breaking of confidentiality and/or intervention:

- I communicate anything that may be interpreted as a threat to self-inflict physical harm.
- I communicate an intention to harm another person.
- I reveal any knowledge of ongoing sexual or physical abuse committed against me or others.
- I exhibit an impaired mental state.
- If I am a legal adult, I reveal that I am sexually involved with a minor or the abuse of a minor.
- I reveal that I am aware of or considering an act of child abuse or child molestation.
- I reveal that I am aware of or considering an abusive act toward an elderly person or persons with handicaps.

The group leaders are committed to maintaining confidentiality. However, I have been advised that for my protection and the protection of potential victims, group leaders may need to break confidentiality if they have concerns about the above types of information and believe I might be in danger of hurting myself or others, or am aware of the threat of harm to others. In cases like these, reports may be made to the proper authorities – police, suicide units, services to children and families, as well as to potential victims. I further acknowledge that if I am under the supervision of adult or youth authorities, part of recovery may include the need to notify these authorities of my involvement in group. If I am a legal adult on probation and/or parole and I engage in wrongful behavior in violation of my parole/probation, part of my healing and recovery may include notification to the proper authorities.

I understand that this is a Christ-centered group, which integrates recovery tools with the Bible and prayer, and that all members may not be of my particular church background. I realize that the Bible may be discussed more or less than I would like it to be.

I realize that this is a support group, and not a therapy group. I understand that the group leader is qualified by "life experience," and not by professional training as a therapist. The leader's role in this group is to create a climate where healing may occur and to support my personal recovery work.

Print Name _____

Signature _____ Date _____

_____ Date_____
Parent / Guardian Signature (if applicant is under 18 years old)

Form adapted from *"Memo of Understanding,"* Pure Desire Ministries Intl. www.puredesire.org.

Typical 423 Meeting

423 groups meet weekly throughout the year.

Groups consist of a maximum of 12 people of various ages, vocations, and backgrounds who share this one thing in common: All members of 423 members struggle with sexual sin.

Meetings always begin and end in prayer.

"423 Small Group Guidelines" are read at every meeting.

Meetings consist of a short assigned lesson with the majority of the time spent in open discussion and personal sharing.

Sharing insights from regular devotional Bible reading and personal journaling is an essential part of 423 meetings.

423 members report on the previous week's successes and failures with sexual sin and lust.

Each member will be asked to establish and share his personal sexual sobriety line with the members of the group.

A 423 group helps to hold each member accountable to remain above his own sexual sobriety line during meetings.

Every member of 423 will be given an opportunity to share his personal story of struggle with sexual sin.

Each individual is expected to fully and honestly disclose the nature of his sexual sin.

No one is allowed to cross-talk, offer advice, or preach at other members of the group. This is a subtle way of introducing shame and judgment.

423 meetings offer a safe and grace-filled environment for members to confess their sexual sin with others in recovery who offer empathy, compassion, mercy, and strength.

When members see each other in a public place outside a 423 meeting, they do not reveal to others their connection to the 423 recovery program.

What is shared in a 423 group remains there. A member who intentionally breaks confidentiality by revealing personal information to people who are not part of the group may be asked to leave 423.

423 Men: If married or engaged, members fully and honestly confess their history of sexual sin to their wives and fiancées. Initial disclosure of this kind should be made early in the recovery process after prayer, careful preparation, and wise counsel from group leaders.

423 Young Men: Members are encouraged to share their history of sexual sin with their parents or guardians if they believe their home is a safe environment for disclosure of this kind.

When a member has achieved and maintained sexual sobriety, and exhibits leadership skills, he may be invited to consider becoming a leader in 423.

423 Small Group Guidelines
(to be read at every meeting)

CONFIDENTIALITY
Nothing that is said or done in this group is ever discussed with people outside the group without the permission of those involved.

SELF-FOCUS
We are here to focus on ourselves, not on others; we share our own experiences, insights, and feelings. We do not offer advice, analyze, or try to "fix" others. All of us are free to find our own answers.

LIMIT SHARING
We are considerate of the need for all to share and we limit our own sharing time accordingly.

REGULAR ATTENDANCE
We agree to be here every week, on time, unless there is an urgent and unavoidable scheduling conflict or genuine emergency. We will call the group leader to explain in advance when we cannot attend or must be late.

HOMEWORK
We are required to complete weekly homework and to participate in small group discussion time.

MAKE CONTACT
We understand the need to be in community and agree to reach out and contact other members throughout the week.

LISTEN RESPECTFULLY
We avoid cross-talk and give each person who shares our undivided attention.

RESPECT OF OTHERS
We guard against offending one another. If someone offends us, or when uncomfortable with anything in this group, we work it out directly with him outside the group instead of expecting others to solve the problem or rescue us.

STAY ON THE SUBJECT
We avoid discussions and debates about controversial topics and outside issues unrelated to healthy sexuality.

SUPPORT
We recognize the need to support Christ's mission of bringing freedom to people bound by sexual addiction. We believe that by giving generously, we strengthen our own journey of recovery as well as help others move toward healthy sexuality.

BEFORE WE LEAVE
When we leave or transfer from our group, we do so respectfully by speaking with our leaders first and then saying goodbye to our group in person to provide proper closure.

LET GOD WORK
We do not preach at or lecture the members of this group.

Form adapted from *"Group Guidelines,"* Pure Desire Ministries Intl. www.puredesire.org.

423 "Cycle of Shame"

You are not alone

Many men feel isolated because of their struggle with sexual sin. "If others really knew my struggle, they would reject me. If my wife [or girlfriend] knew, she would leave me." With nowhere to turn, those who struggle in secrecy rarely find victory.

The enemy of our soul keeps us isolated so we believe the lies: "No one will understand. No one is as bad as me. I will never overcome this. I am beyond help. I am worthless." The Bible calls the devil *"a liar and the father of lies"* (John 8:44). He *"prowls around like a roaring lion, seeking someone to devour"* (1st Peter 5:8). Sexual immorality is one of his oldest and most destructive tools.

- Culture has consistently eroded the traditional role of men and fathers.
- 50–70% of Christian boys and men struggle at some level with sexual purity.
- Internet pornography is accessible, affordable, and anonymous.

Together there is hope

423 can make a difference. It is a safe, confidential environment where we allow God's grace, not guilt and shame, to encourage healing.

> *"Therefore, confess your sins to one another,*
> *and pray for one another so that you may be healed."*
> *James 5.16*

Other men and young men are achieving sexual purity…*you can too!*

The elements of change

"Man looks at the outward appearance, but the LORD looks at the heart", (1st Samuel 16:7). Man's method of finding sexual purity is to try harder to change his behavior. However, this 'white knuckle' approach does not work. We cannot simply stop 'acting out'. Jesus taught, *"For out of the heart come evil thoughts"* (Matthew 15:19). These thoughts cause a person to act impure, because his behavior is tied to his thoughts, and his thoughts come directly from his heart. If our heart is set on the gratification of our wrong sexual desires, our thoughts will conform to our heart's craving, and we will not live consistently pure lives. We must guard our hearts!

> *"Guard you heart with all diligence,*
> *for from it flow the springs of life."*
> *Proverbs 4.23*

As we journey toward sexual purity, we must be honest about our heart longings, asking God to renew us from the inside out. If our heart's desire is to please and honor God, then our thought patterns will steadily move in that direction. As our thought patterns change, so will our behavior. We must be patient. It will take time, but *we can change*.

423 is all about the journey toward heart change.

The cycle of shame

Shame: Many people confuse guilt and shame. Guilt is about what we *do*. Shame is about who we *are*. Shame is our internal assessment that we are bad, flawed, or worthless and leads to emotional pain that cannot be ignored.

Pain: It is difficult for a person to identify pain in their lives. Often it looks like loneliness, inadequacy, panic, hopelessness, and particularly anger. For many of us, addictive sexual activity becomes our only relief from emotional pain.

Wrong Sexual Pleasure: Unfortunately, wrong sexual behavior is an effective medicating device. It *works!* Our pain goes away… but only for a short time. Our body releases naturally occurring drugs called dopamine, similar in makeup to morphine, though even more powerful. Our pain relief is short lived and replaced with deep toxic shame and destructive thoughts like, "I'm defective. I'll never change. I'm worthless!"

The cycle begins again.

The downward spiral

The cycle of shame causes a need for greater levels of pain medication as we build up a tolerance to dopamine. As we engage in stronger 'doses' of sexual sin, our addiction, shame, and pain continue to grow. In our pursuit of a 'better sexual high', we may engage in riskier sexual pleasures. Our sense of separation from God widens and we are tempted to fully surrender to the power of sin. We know we are on the path of destruction, yet we become adept at denying the truth even to ourselves.

Breaking the cycle of shame

There is a way to break this downward spiral, but it cannot be done in secret. Healing is only possible God's way. We must humble ourselves by confessing our sin to the Lord *and* to other people in recovery according to James 5:16. The power Jesus Christ, coupled with the support of trustworthy brothers in recover standing beside us, can break the cycle of shame.

There is hope!

423 Men Leader Qualifications and Responsibilities

Qualifications:

1. You are a Christian, having been baptized as a believer according to the Biblical pattern, and seek to be a fully dedicated follower of Jesus Christ.

2. You meet with Jesus regularly in the practice of prayer, Bible reading, and journaling.

3. You are an active and supportive member of a local church and regularly attend a weekly worship gathering.[69]

4. Your wife (if married) is supportive of your decision to be a leader in 423 Men and fully aware of your history of sexual sin.

5. You have a written sexual sobriety line which you have shared with the members of your 423 Men group.

6. You consistently, though perhaps not perfectly, live above your sexual sobriety line. If you fall seriously below your sexual sobriety line, you are willing to temporarily step aside from 423 Men leadership for a time of self-focus and healing.

7. You have attended a minimum of eight 423 Men Meetings.

8. You have experienced both the bondage and victory of sexual sin and have a passion to serve men stuck in the cycle of sexual addiction.

9. You have authorized a "423 Agreement" and fully support the "423 Small Group Guidelines."

10. You have read *The Pursuit of Porneia*, and subscribe to its tenants.

---

[69] 423 Men began in September 2009 as a ministry of a local church, Solid Rock in Tigard, Oregon. As the church grew and planted other churches, 423 Men also expanded its ministry beyond Solid Rock and now serves a number of local churches as a 501 (c) (3) non-profit organization. This ministry remains true to the standard of local membership. 423 Men leaders are expected to belong to and fully support a local church which holds a high view of Scripture (2nd Timothy 3.16), elevates the person and work of Jesus Christ (1st Corinthians 2.2), and endeavors to be led by the Holy Spirit (Romans 8.14).

Responsibilities:

1. You attend a monthly 423 Men Leaders meeting and maintain excellent and healthy communication with the appointed leadership of the 423 Men recovery program.

2. You are available to lead a 423 Men group with one other co-leader in the manner described in "Typical 423 Meeting." You start and finish your 423 Men meetings on time, arriving early to make certain the room is properly set up.

3. You are willing and available to prepare a weekly lesson and coordinate all elements of a 423 Men meeting in consultation with your co-leader.

4. You ensure that all members of your 423 Men group are allowed to share within the time frame of a two hour meeting.

5. You help to conduct 423 Men intake interviews when asked and as your schedule allows.

6. You receive new men in your group who have completed 423 Men intake interviews when there is space available in your group.

7. You demonstrate compassion for weaker brothers who continue to struggle with the cycle of sexual addiction and pray regularly for the members of your 423 Men group.

8. You do your best to support the individual men in your group and help hold them accountable to "423 Men Guidelines." You willingly and quickly refer the men in your group to other more qualified counselors when that becomes necessary.

9. You are an example of victory over sexual sin but always willing to transparently and honestly share your own current struggles and failures with the men in the 423 Men group you lead.

10. Your goal is to leave the men you lead in better condition than you found them. In that spirit, you do not leave your post as a 423 leader without first making a genuine effort to find and recommend your leadership replacement.

What are Grounds for Stepping Aside from 423 Men Leadership?

"You consistently, though perhaps not perfectly, live above your sexual sobriety line. If you fall seriously below your sexual sobriety line, you are willing to temporarily step aside from 423 Men leadership for a time of self-focus and healing." [70]

Scripture (i.e., Genesis 2.24, 1st Corinthians 6.16-18, Hebrews 13.4, etc.) teaches that guilt-free sex with another person happens only between one man and one woman within the confines of the marital union. In the context of the sacred covenant of marriage, sex is an unparalleled gift from God. 423 Men leaders are called to uphold this Biblical standard and model the God-ordained wonder, beauty, and sanctity of sex by their personal example of holiness.

There is a general minimum sexual sobriety standard to which all 423 Men leaders must adhere. If a leader directly involves another person in his sexual misconduct, this will be considered a serious fall and automatically require the leader to "step aside... for a time of self-focus and healing." Involving another person includes such activities as going to a strip club or adult book store, a one night stand, sex with a prostitute, paying for a sexual massage, web cam computer sex, sexual intercourse with a girlfriend or fiancée, flirtation leading to an emotional affair, homosexual encounter, in short, any form of wrong sexual contact with a live person or actual, physical fornication or adultery.

This restriction in no way condones so-called lesser or more common infractions such as the practice of masturbation while viewing internet pornography or pornographic magazines, use of "soft" pornography, sexualizing women, double-takes and second looks, uncontrolled lustful thoughts, movies with female nudity, sexual fantasies, etc. A leader guilty of this 'adultery of the heart' described by Jesus in Matthew 5.27-28 must distinguish between a

---

[70] Qualification # 6 from *"423 Men Leader Qualifications and Responsibilities."*

lapse (rare occurrence) and a relapse (consistent pattern of failure). If the leader is in a frequent pattern of relapse, then he should also temporarily step aside, even though his sin does not directly engage with or involve another living person. It is always appropriate for a leader to speak with the relapsing co-leader and suggest stepping aside when necessary. For this reason, you should identify and develop trustworthy men in your group as support leaders who can join our leadership team and fill in for co-leaders who "step aside... for a time of self-focus and healing."

A co-leader who "steps aside" should develop a strong relapse prevention plan in consultation with other 423 brothers. Stepping aside is almost always done as a temporary measure with the intention of restoring a brother to active co-leadership according to Galatians 6.1 as soon as possible after repentance and healing take place. When a co-leader "step[s] aside from 423 Men leadership for a time of self-focus and healing," he is not stepping *down* from co-leadership, but rather stepping *aside* to support leadership. The reason he temporarily trades places with a support leader is made fully known to the members of his 423 Men group and his wife (if married). The recovering leader is expected to remain active in both his weekly 423 Men group and the larger, monthly 423 Leaders' group, which acts as a second layer of accountability and support during his "time of self-focus and healing."

James taught, *"Let not many of you become teachers, my brethren, knowing that as such we will incur a stricter judgment"* (James 3.1). 423 leaders are called to a higher standard than 423 members. Paul encouraged his disciple Timothy to *"take pains with these things; be absorbed in them, so that your progress will be evident to all"* (1st Timothy 4.15).

As 423 Men leaders, we know we are not perfect, but we willingly surrender ourselves to Jesus Christ and *"take pains"* to make our *"progress... evident to all."*

"Sharing Your Week" Guidelines

Some groups begin their meetings with the "sharing of weeks." This practice encourages the 423 members to confess their sins and, when coupled with prayer in their community of faith, experience the healing spoken of in James 5.16. With renewed hearts, members are often more receptive to the truths addressed in the weekly homework during the second half of the meeting. During "weeks," it is a good idea to set a timer so each participant will have approximately the same amount of time to speak.

1. State your name and your sexual sobriety line.

Your line should be focused, mainly on sexual sobriety. It will evolve as you grow in your sexual sobriety.

2. Did you remain above or fall below your sobriety line?

If you fell below your line, explain to the group when and where you were below your line. How frequent was this sexual activity? Do you recognize a pattern to this behavior?

If your remained above your sexual sobriety line, to what do you attribute your victory? Were you tempted? How did you deal successfully with your temptations?

3. Ask and answer for yourself the question "Why?"

Each instance of being below your line may have its unique reasons (e.g., underlying negative emotion, childhood trauma, stressor, conflict, disappointment, loss, etc.). Try to be specific in your self-discovery. Share with the members of your group what you plan to do to guard your heart in the coming week. Are there any changes you need to make to your line?

4. Please allow others in the group to ask clarifying questions about your week during the allotted time.

STUDY QUESTIONS

The following sample questions are intended for use in 423 Men group discussions. They are open-ended and designed to help members 'dig deep' into their individual histories of sexual addiction and engage together in the journey of self-discovery. Each member is expected to read the assigned pages and come to group prepared to participate in conversation with his brothers in recovery. It is not possible to cover all weekly questions in forty-five minutes of group dialogue. They are merely a springboard into an experience of quality interaction with the guys in group. It is more important that every member contribute to the discussion in a meaningful way than to power through all study questions. Leaders should pre-read the material, then select the best questions and, as the Holy Spirit leads, adapt them for the particular needs of the men in their 423 Men groups.

Initial Meeting:

Review the Table of Contents and read the "Preface" out loud together in group. Then pose the following questions for group discussion.

1. What titles in the "Table of Contents" most intrigued you or piqued your interest? Why? What do you imagine this section of the book will be about?

2. Where does the name 423 Men come from? Why do you think this Scripture verse was used in the naming of 423 Men? How does this verse personally apply to your desire for sexual sobriety? Memorize and repeat this verse to yourself often.

3. What are "two critical truths" the author learned in the early years of his sexual recovery? Can you relate to these "truths"? Why or why not? Restate these "truths" in your own words and expand on their meaning and application in your own life.

4. What is the "all-important question" we must ask ourselves on the journey of sexual recovery? Why do you think it may be important to pose this question? How does the "all-important question" apply to you and your personal recovery process?

5. Do you agree with Dr. Miller's statements about replicating 423 Men for "multiple settings"? Are all people "in a sense addicted to sin"? Are all of us "in bondage to behaviors rooted in coping mechanisms we've developed as an alternative to confession and repentance"? Please explain.

Week 1:

Read Chapter 1 – "The Journey of Self-Discovery"

1. If 423 Men is not about stopping our bad sexual behavior, then what *is* 423 Men about? Do you agree with the author's premise regarding the purpose of 423 Men? Why or why not?

2. Only one person can make the guy addicted to sex get better. Who is that? Have you or others ever tried 'shame' as a technique to stop your bad sexual behavior? Did it work? Please explain.

3. If the guys in his recovery group cannot make an addict give up his addiction, why then should he attend a 423 Men group? Can his brothers in recovery help a man achieve sexual sobriety? If so, how?

4. What is the author referring to when he uses the term πορνεία? What types of πορνεία have you been involved with? What were the results of your pursuit of πορνεία?

5. What is the journey of self-discovery? How does it apply to our recovery from sexual addictive behavior patterns?

6. Why don't simple answers to the problem of addictions work? Describe a time when you felt judged by a person who gave you a simplistic answer to a personal problem you entrusted that person with. Or, tell about a time when you offered a simple solution to another person's complex problem. What was the result?

7. Should a prospective member attend an actual meeting to determine whether or not the program is a good fit before committing to 423 Men? Please explain.

8. How long does Dr. Ted Roberts say recovery from sexual addiction will typically take if a man is committed to the recovery process? Do you agree or disagree? How long do you think it will take before you are experiencing good sexual sobriety? Please give an explanation for your answer.

9. In your own words, state the two main reasons the author believes an addict should ask himself, "Why am I acting out sexually?" According to the writer, what is the best time for a man to pose the "Why?" question to himself? Why is that a good time to do so?

10. Why is hope important in the recovery process? Have you ever felt hopeless? If so, prepare to tell the group about that experience. Did hopelessness play a role in your addictive behavior patterns? How does a man find hope?

Week 2:

Read Chapter 2 – "The Cycle of Shame"

1. What is the cycle of shame? Describe it in your own words. Can you relate? Explain.

2. Describe your personal experiences with emotional pain. Talk about a time you were suffering emotionally but tried to hide it. How did that experience make you feel?

3. How would you briefly describe your childhood and your family of origin? Share an episode from your adolescent or younger years that impacted the way you think and act today.

4. What are the two kinds of addictions described by the author? Have you ever used addictive chemicals or exhibited addictive behaviors as a response to emotional pain? If so, describe an incident when that occurred.

5. When did sexual curiosity begin for you? Describe the memory of your earliest sexual thought or experience. Can you tell the group how you felt at the time this event took place?

6. Is guilt a 'good thing'? Why or why not? How does guilt differ from shame? Please describe personal experiences with both.

7. Do you have a hard time forgiving yourself? Tell the group of an incident where you needed to forgive yourself. Were you successful? How long do negative self-feelings linger after you sin with πορνεία?

8. The author states, "There was no essential difference between the actions of Peter and Judas." Do you agree with this premise? If you disagree, please give your reasons. Why do you think each disciple's story ends so differently?

9. What two character qualities distinguish every man in active recovery? Why is this so? Do you possess these qualities? Do you see them in your brothers in recovery? Please describe.

10. Why does the author refer to the practice of addiction as "slow suicide"? What keeps the addict on the road to personal destruction? Is suffering necessary for healing?

11. What is redemptive suffering? Can you describe an experience of redemptive suffering in your life?

Week 3:

Read Chapter 3 – "Recovery Myths"

1. Is it hard for you to ask for assistance? Why or why not? Was it difficult for you to seek help in 423 Men? Please describe the emotions you felt as you made the decision to join this recovery group.

2. Have you ever made and broken a promise to remain pure? Did this happen often? How did you respond to your failure before you entered recovery? Can self-confidence undermine the recovery process? Please explain.

3. Do you believe that you are powerless to overcome the spirit of πορνεία? When a man feels powerless to stop sinning sexually, what are his options?

4. Can you name some Christian variations to the "try harder" theme? What are they? Do they work? Why or why not?

5. What is "traditional accountability" according to the author? How does it differ from true recovery? Can attendance at a weekly accountability meeting be detrimental to an addict's recovery? What is meant by "binge and purge"? How does the addict benefit from this practice?

6. Explain the myth of God-dependency in your own words. Is it possible to depend on God too much, or in a false way that undermines His purpose in your life? Please describe.

7. What role does obedience play in the life of a man who is truly dependent on God? Please tell the group about a time that you sensed clear direction from the Lord. Did you obey or disobey? What was the result?

8. Fill in the blanks: "Without God, I _____. Without me, He _____." What does this phrase mean to you? Do you believe this saying is true? Why or why not?

9. Do addicts lie? Have you ever lied about your addictive patterns of sexual misbehavior? According to the author, "heresy is partial truth, or truth mixed with lies." What are the half-truths you have told yourself and others?

10. God's nature remains a mystery (Isaiah 55.9). He is free to act in ways that surprise, baffle, perplex, disappoint, and even outrage us. Has your journey of recovery thus far taken unpredictable or surprising turns which you can share with the group?

Week 4:

Read Chapter 4 – "Addiction Takes You Somewhere You Don't Want to Go"

1. What is meant by "a progressive sin"? Is the pursuit of πορνεία a progressive sin? Is it possible to "manage" our sexually addictive behaviors (e.g., plateau at an acceptable level of routine 'minor' sexual infractions)? Why or why not?

2. Have you made excuses for your sexual activities? If so, please share some of your common ones with the group. Have you ever looked at another man's sin and concluded, "I'm not *that* bad. I would never do anything like *that*." What are the potential problems associated with that type of thinking?

3. Addictive behaviors cause the addict to become more sensitized to his drug of choice. Describe the brain process of "sensitization" as it applies to sexual sin. How does "sensitization" differ from "tolerance" to sexual stimuli?

4. According to data quoted by the author, more than half of high school aged people have smart phones. Is that a smart idea? Why or why not?

5. Do you wish to leave this world a better place than you found it? If so, share with the group specific ways you are trying to do that. (Please pray and spend some thoughtful time on this one.)

6. What is PIED? Do you believe PIED is a real phenomenon? Have you ever experienced it, or know anyone who has? For those who are not sexually active, how does the prospect of PIED make you feel about sex in your future?

7. Have you heard of new secular organizations and books dealing with effects of pornography (e.g., Fight the New Drug, Reboot Nation, Your Brain on Porn, NoFap Reddit, WACK, etc.)? Does the church have an obligation to educate followers of Jesus in a similar way? Please explain.

8. According to the author, what is the key difference between John Mayer in 2010 and Christian men in unhappy, sexless marriages who use pornography? Is this observation an indictment on these men, the culture of the church, both, neither? Defend your answer.

9. When it comes to your sexual addictive behavior patterns, have you ever felt like two persons in one? If so, how did your 'dual personality' feelings affect your relationships with friends and loved ones?

10. In 423 Men we have a saying, "You can't get clean until you come clean." Is it possible to experience true intimacy without exposing your secrets? Please explain.

Week 5:

Read Chapter 5 – "You Can Recover, But Not Alone"

1. If Jesus is the answer to the problem of πορνεία, why do the majority of men who follow Him, according to the statistic quoted in Chapter 4, view online pornography at least monthly? Please avoid a simplistic answer like, "Because we are all sinners."

2. What is the historical context of the Scriptural premise, "I can do all things through Him who strengthens me" (Philippians 4.13)? Can this verse be used as a mask for self-reliance in the arena of recovery from sex addiction?

3. What is the difference between anonymity and confidentiality? Do you feel safe in your 423 Men group? Tell the group about a time your trust was violated. Did you feel betrayed?

4. Trust is hard to establish and easy to lose. How do we earn trust in 423 Men? What are the "Two C's" and how do they play a role in the building of trust in a group setting?

5. If we can't give or receive advice and wise counsel in group, then what's the point of meeting together?

6. What does the author mean when he refers to a "Cultural Shift in the Church"? In regard to sexual recovery, have you seen a shift in your church? What can you do to help your local church in this transition? Does your attitude and approach to church leaders play a role in the success of recovery ministry? Please explain.

7. What is the "fizzle factor" as it pertains to recovery groups. Have you ever tried to get accountability with a small group of friends? Did it work? How did that experience compare with your involvement in 423 Men?

8. What, in the author's opinion, is the primary reason for a highly structured approach to recovery? Do you agree? Why or why not?

9. If you were offered a magical pill that would keep you from ever again mentally visualizing a naked woman (other than your wife, if married), would you take it? What is the real reason treatment for sexual recovery often fails, according to the writer? Would you opt to live in a world without πορνεία? Be real in your answer.

Week 6:

Read Chapter 6 – "Interrupting the Pattern of Relapse"

1. Is there a difference between a "momentary lapse" and a "pattern of relapse" in sexual addiction? Have you recognized a pattern of relapse in your sexual behaviors? If so, please describe. What is "stabilization" in the context of sexual recovery (and as defined by the author)?

2. "In sexual recovery, a man needs a standard by which to measure his progress." Do you agree with this statement? Why or why not? Does strict adherence to our sobriety line equate to, or play a role in, personal holiness? Please explain your answer.

3. Is it important to have a clearly written "relapse prevention plan"? Do you have one? Why or why not? What are some key components of an effective "relapse prevention plan"?

4. Does admission of failure to others act as a deterrent to future sin? What are some other deterrents to your pattern of relapse? Is deterrence effective?

5. Is addiction the same as sin? If you feel there is a distinction between sin and addiction, please describe. Have you ever used your addiction as an excuse for sin?

6. Name five ways an addict lies. (See section entitled "Plausible Deniability.") Tell the men in your group about a time when you lied in one of these ways.

7. What are two ways in which self-lies are accomplished? Have you ever lied to yourself in one of these two ways? What is plausible deniability? Give an example. Why do addicts sometimes engage in this form of self-deception?

8. What is meant by "trolling" in the context of sexual recovery? Have you ever set yourself up for an 'accidental hit' of πορνεία? Talk about it with the group.

9. In Hebrews 2.1 NIV the writer states, "We must pay careful attention, therefore, to what we have heard, so that we do not drift away." Does the power of "drift" affect your sobriety? How? What remedies you have found helpful in resisting a tendency to "drift away" from your convictions?

10. What are some benefits to walking in sexual freedom? You may refer to the list near the end of Chapter 6, but also share from your own experience with sexual sobriety.

Week 7:

Read Chapter 7 – "Marital Disclosure"

1. Do you consider the pursuit of πορνεία to be a violation of a man's wedding vows? Is a man 'cheating' on his wife when he views pornography? Please explain.

2. Do you believe that it is imperative to fully disclose your history of sexual sin to your wife or fiancée? What if your wife or fiancée tells you she does not want to know about your sexual infractions? Does her apparent disinterest relieve you from the need to disclose?

3. Is it possible to keep secrets in marriage? Why or why not? How does your answer square with Luke 8.17? Should your wife act as your accountability partner? Can you see potential problems with that arrangement? Please describe.

4. Define marital intimacy in your own words. Can you have intimacy without honesty? Please explain.

5. Is a man's failure to disclose his sexual history with his wife a form of dishonesty? Please defend your answer.

6. What precautions should a husband take before disclosing his history of sexual sin to his wife for the first time? Is the concern of hurting a man's wife a valid reason to delay or choose not to make full disclosure to her?

7. Is partial disclosure of a husband's sexual history helpful or harmful to the marital relationship? What are some potential problems associated with telling a wife some, but not all, of the truth?

8. Fill in the blanks: "Nakedness is ___ _____ concept long before it is ___ _____ one. Great sex is not characterized by _____ nakedness, but by naked _____ between a man and a woman in holy matrimony." What are your thoughts about these statements?

9. What is the goal of marriage, according to the author? Is his premise supportable by the Scriptural idea of marriage found in Genesis 2.24? Offer your own thoughts.

10. What characterizes "guilt-free" sex? How does this type of sex differ from other forms of sex? What is "cheap sex," according to the author? Does God promise "an

unlimited supply of "guilt-free" sex throughout your life? How does your answer make you feel?

Week 8:

Read Chapter 8 – "The Battle for Emotional Survival"

1. Recall a personal conflict you had with another person. Could that conflict have played a role in your sexual addictive behavior pattern? Describe the conflict to your group. (Be careful not to offer information that may be traceable to those you were in conflict with.)

2. Do you think an attempt toward reconciliation with difficult people could be helpful to your sexual sobriety? Please elaborate. How do you feel when you are successful in making peace with an adversary?

3. Name at least two reasons Jesus ordered his followers to "make friends quickly" with their opponents? Look at the list of five Scriptures about peace and interaction with our enemies near the beginning of Chapter 8. Which of these Bible texts speaks to you most profoundly? Why?

4. As an adolescent, did you ever talk to your parents about your sexual temptations? If so, how did it go? If not, why not, and how do you surmise the conversation would have gone?

5. Did you ever feel abused or neglected as a child? Have you forgiven or considered forgiving the perpetrators? Who does forgiveness benefit? How does that benefit take place?

6. After Jacob's encounter with God, "he was limping." What are your thoughts about the author's premise that Jacob's limp "was representative of the pain he had to suffer to become the man he was destined to be...

Israel." Can you make an application of Jacob's experience in your own life?

7. At what precise point in time, according to the author, did Esau experience the fulfillment of his father, Isaac's blessing recorded in Genesis 27.39-40? In your experience, can unforgiveness feel like a heavy burden or "yoke"?

8. Sometimes we are hurt accidentally and without malice by people who, like you, are in their own battle for emotional survival. Does searching for common ground with these people make it easier to forgive them? Please explain.

9. Explain the author's "relational log jam" analogy in your own words. What normally results from "log picking" or "dynamite" in dealing with broken relationships?

Week 9:

Read Chapter 9 – "Embrace the Darkness"

1. "Addicts," according to the author, "are skilled in pain avoidance." Have you used sex as a way to keep from feeling emotional pain? Please describe an actual incident of this kind to the group.

2. To suffer redemptively means, according to the writer, "to suffer with hope and a determination to learn from our trauma." Can you describe an experience of learning from your emotional pain?

3. Is self-awareness on the journey of recovery enough to keep an addict sexually sober? Can a man be aware of the underlying reasons for his sexual misbehavior and still continue to act out sexually? What are his next steps in the recovery process?

4. God promises you a way out of temptation "so that you can endure" (1st Corinthians 10.13). Does God's 'way out' always involve suffering? Can you escape temptation without feeling some level of emotional pain?

5. According to Hebrews 2.17-18, Jesus suffered when He was tempted. Check out Hebrews 4.15 and discuss the following question with your group: Was Jesus tempted to pursue πορνεία? Did Jesus, like you and me, suffer with sexual temptation? Is Jesus sympathetic of the addict's plight?

6. Describe Jerry Sittser's "setting sun" analogy (from *A Grace Disguised*). Does this illustration apply to your battle with addiction? If so, please share your insights.

7. Why must we "embrace the darkness" of our own suffering? Are there alternatives to suffering? If so, what are they?

8. The writer states, "The objective is not to avoid emotional pain, but rather to learn from it." Do you agree? What have you learned from your suffering? Has your "darkness" made you a better human?

9. Can you ever fully identify with or truly feel another man's emotional pain? Is it necessary to do so in order to assist him on his journey of recovery?

10. In your opinion, which is the better question to ask: "Why must I suffer?" or "Why do I suffer?" Please explain your answer.

Week 10:

Read Chapter 10 – "A New Passion"

1. Jesus said, "...anyone who looks at a woman lustfully has already committed adultery with her in his heart" (Matthew 5.27 NIV). Have you ever been guilty of 'adultery of the heart'? Is it possible for you to look at an attractive woman and acknowledge her beauty without lusting for her?

2. Is it reasonable to think we can avoid the temptation of πορνεία? Do you agree with the author's premise that because we are 'in the world' and share the planet with beautiful women, we must learn to appreciate both their inner and outer beauty? Please explain your answer.

3. What is the goal of sexual sobriety, according to the author? How are we are to treat women, according to the Bible?

4. Go over each item in both columns on the "Sexualization Chart." Which column better describes your typical approach toward beautiful people of the opposite sex? Are you making headway toward the column on the left? Please describe.

5. Are you showing mercy to yourself and others in the area of sexual sobriety? Are you able to forgive yourself when you fall, and make an immediate comeback? Discuss with your group a recent personal experience with showing or receiving mercy.

6. Who is the real enemy? What are some common strategies in fighting this enemy? In your opinion, what is the best strategy in stopping this foe?

7. Is it possible to stop πορνεία in your life? In the lives of others? In society at large? Can we "kill the porn industry" as the author suggests? Why or why not?

8. Who is responsible for the existence of published pornography? Is it fair to say that private porn use hurts no one? Why or why not?

9. Have you considered your influence? The Apostle Paul told his audience at the Corinthian church, "I urge you to imitate me" (1st Corinthians 4.16). When it comes to use of pornography in the media, can you state with confidence to other men, "I urge you to imitate me"? Would you like to?

10. What do you want more... πορνεία or an active and effective ministry serving humanity in the name of Jesus? Is it possible to have both? Why or why not?

Final Week:

Read "Afterword" and pose the following questions regarding the subject of 423 Men leadership for group discussion.

1. Are 423 Men groups Bible studies? Complete this phrase: "The goal of recovery is not information, but _____." Is it possible for a man to have an excellent grasp of Scripture, and still be stuck in sexual sin? Please explain.

2. Does the Bible speak to the issue of healthy sexuality? What's your favorite verse that deals with the main subject matter in *The Pursuit of Porneia*? Do you practice P. B. & J.? If so, please share a recent insight you gleaned from your P. B. & J.

3. What are the main elements of an effective 423 Men meeting? What is your favorite part of the group you attend? Why did you join 423 Men? Why do you remain in this recovery program?

4. Have you shared your "personal story of struggle with sexual sin" with the guys in group? Are you preparing to do so?

5. Is 423 Men therapy? What is the main difference between a therapy group and a recovery group? Do all men with sexually addictive behavior patterns need a recovery group? Do they all need therapy in addition to group? Please explain your answers.

6. Do you respect the men in your group? Do you feel respected by these men? Why or why not? Can you list several ways the guys in group may demonstrate respect to each other? What are some reasons, according to the author, that every man respect-worthy?

7. Is attendance at weekly 423 Men meetings mandatory or optional? Why do you think there is a 423 Men guideline regarding attendance?

8. What are the two main dangers of advice-giving in a 423 Men meeting? Is there such a thing as 'good advice'? How and when may we offer or receive counsel, a 'word from God', or advice? According to the author, "Cheap advice is the worst form of condescension, and we must avoid it at all costs." Do you agree or disagree? Why?

9. What is the distinction between co-leaders and support leaders in 423 Men? Do leaders teach or facilitate? What is the difference? 423 Men leaders are expected to gently shut down over-talkers and warmly draw out shy guys. Is this procedure helpful to the success of a typical 423 Men group? Why or why not?

10. What is meant by Jude's mandate to the early church: *"And have mercy on those who doubt; save others by snatching them out of the fire..."* Jude 23 ESV? Does this verse motivate you to help others on the journey of sexual sobriety?

ACKNOWLEDGMENTS

I am enormously indebted to Dr. Debi Miller for her gracious gift of untold hours spent in reviewing manuscripts, correcting grammar, and strengthening the readability of *The Pursuit of Porneia.*

I first met Dr. Miller in a meeting of concerned citizens brainstorming ideas to help young men resist sexual temptations within easy reach of their smart phones. I informed the group of the book I was working on and Debi offered her assistance. I took her up on her gracious offer and she read my fifty-five thousand word manuscript, not once, but twice, in detail. Her suggested revisions, margin notes, and constant encouragement kept me in the writing game. Thank you, Coach Miller!

Debi holds her doctorate in education from George Fox University and has worked in Christian education for thirty years. Her impressive resume includes the co-founding of a Christian high school, creation of a teacher education program at Multnomah University, and serving as the Principal of Westside Christian High School in Tigard, Oregon. Dr. Miller and her husband Roger, also a lifetime educator, have been married thirty-three years and reside in Vancouver, Washington.

I am overwhelmingly grateful for the encouragement of two mentors, Ted Roberts of Pure Desire International, Gresham, Oregon, and Dick Iverson, "my father in the faith" and founder of City Bible Church, Portland, Oregon. I probably would not be alive today without the loving intervention and influence of these mighty men of God. I am also grateful to my many other "friends for life," including the pastors and elders at Westside and A Jesus Church and the entire A Jesus Church Network, the many leaders of 423 Men groups, my friends, my children, and my extended family. Thank you for standing by me and the ministry of 423 Communities International.

I will always cherish the memory of my wife, Adonica. She was a big fan of 423 Men and she never quit believing in the mission. Thank you Jesus for two decades with this wonderful woman.

ABOUT THE AUTHOR

Dave Scriven oversees 423 Men, a ministry of 423 Communities, a 501 (c) (3) non-profit organization founded at Westside – A Jesus Church, formerly called Solid Rock in Tigard, Oregon. Over eight hundred men and about two hundred women have actively participated in 423 Communities for sexual recovery since its inception in September, 2009.

Mr. Scriven is a former Presbyterian minister with an M. Div. from the University of Dubuque Theological Seminary and an M. A. in Bible from St. Thomas Aquinas Institute, Iowa, both earned in 1977. He commonly speaks on the subject of sexual recovery and leadership development in communities of faith. 423 Men currently hosts over twenty groups in twelve locations, including Bridgetown Church in Portland, Oregon, and Van City Church in Vancouver, Washington, with an active weekly attendance of about two hundred and fifty members.

Dave has seven children and seven grandchildren. He is widowed and resides with his youngest teenage daughter in Beaverton, Oregon.

Mr. Scriven and his team are enthusiastically available to serve your church and they may be reached at:

Email: info@423communities.org

Website: www.423communities.org

Confidential: (503) 898-0423

Mail: PO Box 1055
                Beaverton, OR 97075

Made in the USA
Coppell, TX
27 June 2021